STRESS MANAGEMENT FOR LAWYERS
by Amiram Elwork

Excerpts From Book Reviews Of First Edition

"This very readable treatise will be of practical use for attorneys, for people who work in the legal field or for anyone who places a high priority on getting things done.......Its appeal lies in its direct, simple style. .... Concepts are explained clearly with examples right from the attorney's work setting."

Jeanne B. Clark, Trial News,
Washington State Trial Lawyers Association

"Every lawyer who reads this primer on stress will learn something constructive about his or her reactions to people, places and particularly the dynamic events of legal practice. Even those who are in denial and claim that their lives are 'stress free' will find it helpful."

Emma R. Stephens,
Michigan Trial Lawyers Association Quarterly

" *Stress Management for Lawyers* is direct, succinct and to-the-point in its advice..........the book's style and organization make it an excellent handout at an in-house seminar."

Paul Warren, Law Letter,
Virginia Trial Lawyers Association

"The best feature of this slender volume is the logical, step-by-step analysis which the author uses to determine what causes stress, the impact that stress has upon our bodies and emotions, and how to react in a positive manner to stressors in our lives."

John Brendon Gately,
Law Practice Management Magazine

"Buying this little book might be the best ...... investment any lawyer can make."

" Clear, concise ...... valuable ...... practical ..... book helps lawyers cope with workplace stress."

"I scrutinized the book before running this review. It's a good book with common sense self-help techniques."

"This volume is different ....particularly appropriate for attorneys ......conclusions and concepts are well annotated."

"We especially liked - and related to - the section on procrastination...... Good advice from a good book."

"It is a good investment for any lawyer in this competitive environment."

"Psychologist and legal educator Dr. Amiram Elwork has done a remarkable job of identifying the major causes of stress in the legal profession. Even more impressively, he has put together a powerful list of remedies in a book that reads very easily."

"*Stress Management for Lawyers* should greatly assist attorneys or managers of law firms in their efforts to maximize the productivity of law practice, while improving the quality of the firm's environment."

Richard A. Waltz,
The Colorado Lawyer

"Even if you only use a small portion of the techniques provided in this manual, the pay-off will be substantial."

Cherie P. Shanteau,
Utah Bar Journal

" the information on the stress-producing thought process (alone) is worth the cost of the book."

James Wilson,
The Nevada Lawyer

"........easy to read and .... contains helpful advice."

Book Editor,
Oklahoma Bar Journal

"Dr. Elwork's book is worth reading.......points out the average lawyer's feelings and remedies for different problems."

Book Editor,
New York State Bar Journal

"I recommend this book as a quick read that can assist lawyers in gaining perspective and facilitating self-analysis....... specific proactive steps are the book's best value and alone make this short book worthy of perusal."

Richard J. King, Jr.,
The Pennsylvania Lawyer

STRESS MANAGEMENT FOR LAWYERS

Second Edition

How To Increase Personal & Professional Satisfaction In The Law

Amiram Elwork, Ph.D.
Law-Psychology Graduate Program
Widener University

With Contributions By

Douglas B. Marlowe, Ph.D., J.D.
Institute For Addictive Disorders
Allegheny University Of The Health Sciences

The Vorkell Group
Gwynedd, Pennsylvania

SEE ORDER FORM ON LAST PAGE

Published by:

The Vorkell Group
P.O. Box 447, Gwynedd, PA 19436
Phone: (215) 661-9330;   Fax: (215) 661-9328
Order Line: (800) 759-1222

The Vorkell Group donates a portion of its book proceeds to college scholarship funds that support talented young people in need of financial aid.

Cover design by John Goschke, Cornerstone Media, Ambler, PA.

Printed in the United States of America
First Edition - First Printing, 1995; Second Printing, 1996
Second Edition - First Printing 1997

Publisher's Cataloging in Publication Data

Elwork, Amiram
    Stress management for lawyers: how to increase personal & professional satisfaction in the law / Amiram Elwork ; with contributions by Douglas B. Marlowe. - 2nd ed.
        p.   cm.
    Includes bibliographic references.
    Library of Congress Catalog Card Number: 96-61265
    ISBN 0-9644727-1-6
    1. Practice of law -- United States -- Psychological aspects.
    2. Lawyers -- Job stress -- United States. 3. Stress
    management.   I. Marlowe, Douglas B.   II. Title.
KF300.Z9 E5 1997   340'.023'019

Dedicated to my daughters,

Rachael and Rebecca.

ACKNOWLEDGMENTS

I greatly appreciate the help of many individuals whose aid and support made this book possible. First, I want to acknowledge the influence that my clients, graduate students, and seminar participants have had on shaping my ideas. Thank you for the opportunity to work with you and for sharing your insights with me.

I want to thank the many book reviewers and letter writers who gave the first edition of this book praise and constructive criticism. You helped guide the creation of this edition. I would like to thank James Hatch, the Director of the Ohio CLE Institute, for suggesting the addition of a section for impaired lawyers. Thank you, Douglas Marlowe, for contributing two chapters to that section. Thank you Paula Barran, Myer Cohen and Don Jones for your critique of the chapter on the legal questions facing impaired lawyers. I would also like to thank Mark Siwik, a fine lawyer and friend; our joint seminars and discussions have inspired me and greatly expanded my horizons.

To Albert Block, Lynn Block, Rachael Elwork and Andrea Elwork, who spent many hours editing and proofreading this book in its manuscript form, I thank you for that and for your caring support. Finally, my wife, Andrea, and my daughters, Rachael and Rebecca, deserve a special thanks for the many sacrifices they have made so that I could bring this project to fruition. Their love gives me the courage to take risks and the energy to be creative.

Amiram Elwork

Things do not change, we do.

Henry David Thoreau

CONTENTS

SECTION I

INTRODUCTION

Happiness is not a destination.
It is a method of life.

Burton Hillis

It is not easy to find happiness
in ourselves, and yet
it is not possible to find
it elsewhere.

Agnes Repplier

AN INVITATION TO PURSUE HAPPINESS

The practice of law has become an increasingly difficult occupation. The evidence for this claim is overwhelming. Recent national surveys of lawyers have consistently found rising rates of job dissatisfaction.[1] A significant number of attorneys are dropping out of law and switching to new careers.[2] Even more alarming is the fact that lawyers have unusually high rates of depression, substance abuse and a variety of other mental and physical ailments.[3] Researchers agree that these are not statistical anomalies, but a reflection of how tough it is to be a lawyer today.

For example, take the case of one of my past clients - let's call him J.D. He had read an article I had written for a local legal magazine and decided to call. He was courteous but very direct. Right from the start, he wanted me to know that he did not have much faith in psychologists and doubted that anyone could help him. Out of desperation, however, he was willing to try anything.

His story was familiar. J.D. had started out as a solo practitioner twenty years ago, when all one had to do was hang out a shingle and practice law. Things had become much more competitive and complicated since then. Even though he had other attorneys working for him, J.D. felt unable to slow down. In fact, although he was putting in more hours than ever, his profits were plummeting. After years of putting up with his long hours and hostile mood swings, his wife was threatening to leave him. He was taking several pills - some to help him get to sleep and others to help him face the day. His self-esteem was at an all time low.

Unquestionably, part of J.D.'s problems stemmed from psychological issues that had little to do with being a lawyer. Clearly, however, J.D. also was experiencing a number of occupational stressors. Like most lawyers, he was under relentless time pressures and had more work to do than he could possibly finish. In addition, he was operating under the tension of fierce economic competition, in an adversarial environment that breeds hostility, conflict, and cynicism.

Unfortunately, J.D. did not know how to cope with the many stresses of a law practice in a healthy manner. Similarly, he knew very little about time management, marketing or billing, and he lacked the ability to manage other people. When confronted with these facts, his initial response was, "Why isn't it enough to just practice law?" He greatly resisted the idea that although he was a good lawyer in the traditional sense, the solutions to many of the problems he was experiencing at work required certain skills that he had never learned.

J.D.'s story is not very different from those of other attorneys I have counseled. It is a general fact that few lawyers expend much energy learning to reduce stress. Some believe that there is nothing to this, other than fluff, and that ultimately what makes a successful lawyer is traditional legal competence. Others believe that "you either have it naturally or you don't" and that stress management skills cannot be taught. Attorneys who see the need to learn stress management techniques have yet another problem; these skills receive scant attention in law school and are just beginning to be taught through credit-worthy continuing education seminars.

The time has come for the legal community to officially recognize stress management as an extremely important part of a lawyer's repertoire. Many lawyers are truly in need of the information contained herein. This second edition is an expanded, updated and refined version of the well received first edition. An enormous amount of valuable knowledge is distilled down to its essential and practical elements and applied to the particulars of practicing law.

Lacking stress management skills may be keeping you from achieving your full potential. Learning them will help you experience job satisfaction, achieve a balance between your career and personal life, improve your relationships with associates and clients, and even increase your productivity. Only you, however, have the power to accept my invitation to read this book and use its contents to improve your own health and happiness.

HOW IS THIS BOOK DIFFERENT?

Given the availability of many excellent self-help books,[4] I am often asked how this one is different from the rest. In particular, the questioner usually wants to know whether the last word in the title of the book could be "doctors, accountants, or even plumbers" just as easily as "lawyers?" After all, stress is a universal human problem and it can be understood in terms of general psychological principles.

In answering such a question, I explain that this book *is* qualitatively different from general books about stress. First of all, it contains a number of chapters that pertain particularly to attorneys. Section II, in which I review the research that has been done specifically with lawyers, is a good example of this. In addition, the illustrations used throughout the book are taken right from the legal workplace and are based on the accounts of many lawyers I have interviewed.

Another distinguishing characteristic of this book is that the self-help techniques emphasized are based on my knowledge of what works with attorneys. Any good consultant knows that understanding a client's problems is not enough. Such problems must be explained in ways that the client will find meaningful. In addition, the advice that is offered must be based on what the client is capable of doing or accepting. This type of expertise is subtle, but it often makes the difference between failure and success.

I have attempted to fill this book with subtleties that will help you find it meaningful. For example, I know that a majority of lawyers value reasoned logic, and do not respond well to what are sometimes called "touchy-feely" techniques. As a result, I have purposefully placed greater emphasis on strategies that involve rational analysis and have done my best to explain them in a highly logical, step-by-step fashion.

Obviously, I am not suggesting that you shouldn't read other books. Because it speaks to lawyers so directly, however, reading this book is a good way to start your journey toward greater personal and professional satisfaction. To arrive at this destination, however, you will need to do much more than read this one book. Other books that are suggested throughout the succeeding pages will help expand your knowledge about a variety of issues. In addition, you will have to convert what you have learned into action.

MAKE IT SIMPLE

"Everything should be made as simple as possible,
but not simpler." *Albert Einstein*

My core belief in the elegance of simplicity pervades the structure of this book. Not only is this the way I have approached my writing assignment, it is also what I recommend you do in reading this book and in trying its recommendations.

I am going to help you understand complex concepts and self-help techniques at their most elemental level. Do not be fooled by the fact that some of the advice given will sound like common sense. The problem is that common sense is not so commonly practiced. In addition, do not confuse simplicity with lack of sophistication. Nobel prizes have been awarded to people who have explained complex phenomena in fundamental terms.

While my goals are a bit less lofty, I think that it is extremely important to make very complex issues easy to understand. Simplification makes things more clear, more orderly, more memorable, less overwhelming, and easier to put into practice. In reading this book, do not just learn the basics, over-learn them. Make them a part of your natural thinking process. This way, when faced with the most complex of problems, you will know what to do automatically or at least know how to start.

Given how busy most lawyers are, each chapter is short and succinct, requiring only a few minutes of your attention. Thus, even if your primary complaint is lack of time, you can read this book whenever you have a moment to spare, and still get something out of it each time you open it.

While the chapters are presented in a logical sequence, it is not necessary to read them in that order. Most chapters stand on their own. Therefore, you can turn to any section that happens to be of interest to you at a particular moment and get the needed information quickly.

Finally, this is not the kind of book you read once from cover to cover and never open again. It is written as a reference guide that you can return to repeatedly, whenever you need a refresher or a solution to a specific and immediate problem. Again, brevity and simplicity make it a more inviting resource.

SECTION II

THE PROBLEM:

A PROFESSION

IN DISTRESS

Nothing in life is to be feared. It is only to be understood.

Marie Curie

It is easier to perceive error than to find the truth, for the former lies on the surface and is easily seen, while the latter lies in the depth, where few are willing to search for it.

Johann Wolfgang von Goethe

THE BASIS FOR CONCERN

In April of 1991, the American Bar Association (ABA) convened a conference entitled *At the Breaking Point*. Their report[5] concluded that "there is a growing trend in the legal profession which, left unchecked, threatens the well-being of all lawyers and firms in every part of the country." The trend was a noticeable deterioration of the legal work environment, an accompanying reduction in career satisfaction among lawyers, as well as a significant decrease in their physical and mental health. Although the report focused on the consequences of these developments for lawyers and law firms, it was obvious that litigants and the integrity of the entire legal process were also being affected.

Consequences of Distress On:

Lawyers & Law Firms -*e.g., dissatisfaction, turnover, mental and physical illness, substance abuse, malpractice and health insurance costs*

Litigants & Legal System- *e.g., ethical violations, malpractice, incompetence*

Expressions of concern began more than a decade earlier as numerous legal magazines started to report a meaningful decline in the quality of life among lawyers. In response to such reports, the ABA Young Lawyers Division[6] conducted an in-depth survey of the legal profession in 1984. A random national sample of close to 2,300 attorneys participated. The results suggested that while the earlier reports were somewhat exaggerated, it was still noteworthy that about 15% of the respondents were generally dissatisfied with their jobs. More noteworthy, however, was the fact that even lawyers who were generally satisfied with their careers, reported that their jobs required them to endure high levels of daily pressures and tensions.

In 1990, the ABA Young Lawyers Division[7] conducted a similar follow-up survey with a random national sample of close to 2,200 attorneys. This time, 19% of all attorneys reported being generally dissatisfied with their jobs. This represented a 27% increase in the general level of dissatisfaction reported six years earlier. Over 70% of lawyers in all settings reported that pressure and tension on the job was considerable. Another national survey of over 1200 attorneys, conducted through Temple University,[8] reported that 23% of the respondents were dissatisfied with their jobs in 1992.

In addition to these national surveys, local studies were also conducted. For example, in 1990 the North Carolina Bar Association[9] surveyed close to 2,600 attorneys. Like their national cohorts, over 18% of North Carolina attorneys reported being dissatisfied with their jobs. Even though close to 80% of them were generally satisfied with their lives and careers, they reported unusually high rates of negative psychological and physical symptoms. Close to 37% of them admitted to feeling depressed and over 42% reported feeling lonely in the past few weeks. About 25% reported physical symptoms of depression (e.g., appetite loss, lethargy) and anxiety (e.g., trembling, heart racing). Over 11% reported suicidal ideation at least 1-2 times per month in the past year, and close to 17% reported drinking 3-5 alcoholic beverages per day.

A series of other studies on the health of lawyers have essentially replicated the findings in North Carolina. Using scientifically validated measures of psychopathology, one study[10] demonstrated that the mental health of lawyers begins to deteriorate with their entrance into law school. Whereas students entering the School of Law at The University of Arizona were found to be similar to the general population, by the spring semester they were found to report significantly higher than average rates of psychopathological symptoms, including signs of depression, anxiety, hostility, and paranoia. The symptoms continued to increase into the end of the law school program, and did not return to pre-law school levels within the first two years of legal practice.

Another research study[11] surveyed 801 lawyers in the state of Washington and found alarming rates of reported depression and substance abuse. Again, using validated measures of psychopathology, this study found that 19% of Washington lawyers suffered from depression and 18% were problem drinkers. Given a 5% overlap between the two groups, close to one third of the sample had a significant mental health problem. These figures represented rates that are at least twice the national average for the general population. With no reason to believe that there is something unrepresentative about Washington state lawyers, the researchers concluded that similar rates of depression and problem drinking would be found in most jurisdictions in the United States.

Indeed, a Johns Hopkins University study[12] measured the prevalence of Major Depressive Disorder within a number of occupations across many locations (e.g., New Haven, Baltimore, St. Louis and Los Angeles). Of the 28 occupations that could be compared in a statistically valid manner, lawyers were the most likely to suffer from depression and 3.6 times more likely than average to do so. The researchers concluded that the legal environment may be particularly conducive to depression due to the stress that it produces, and mentioned such factors as work load and job complexity.

The statistics reviewed above suggest that out of approximately 850,000 attorneys in the United States at this time, over 275,000 of them are experiencing significant mental health problems. This explains why the ABA sponsored conference mentioned earlier was entitled *At The Breaking Point*. The title was not hyperbolic. It reflected a recognition by many[13] that an excessive number of lawyers are in distress.

The consequences of this fact go far beyond causing lawyers to experience mental health problems. Chronic stress has been linked to a variety of physical ailments, ranging from headaches to coronary diseases.[14] It can also trigger the deterioration of close personal relationships and contribute to unsuccessful child rearing and failed marriages.

Chronic stress not only damages lawyers and their families, but also affects their ability to serve clients effectively.[15] It has been estimated that 40-75% of the disciplinary actions taken against lawyers involve practitioners who are chemically dependent or mentally ill.[16] While most attorneys never experience serious impairment, even medium levels of chronic stress are likely to have a deleterious effect on their ability to work at peak effectiveness (e.g., meet deadlines, detect emerging problems). Thus, even though most failures by lawyers are not redressed, they still have a significant negative effect on litigants and the integrity of the entire legal system.

This problem also has ramifications for law firms. The health consequences of stress raise health insurance costs and subject law firms to the risk of large law suit awards under various disability statutes. For example, it has been reported that an in-house counsel in San Francisco was awarded over one million dollars "because his company refused to 'accommodate' his depression by agreeing to shorter hours" or taking other supportive measures.[17]

Stress has been linked to high rates of absenteeism and staff turnover. Statistics show that every year a significant number of lawyers either leave their firms or the practice of law altogether.[18] Finally, stress has been linked to the costs that law firms suffer as a result of malpractice cases brought against them.[19]

WHY IS LAW SO STRESSFUL?

In a scholarly book[20] about the state of the legal profession in the late twentieth century, Mary Ann Glendon asks, "Why are so many lawyers so sad?" To understand the answer to Professor Glendon's question, we need to acknowledge its complexity. Clearly, the fact that lawyers suffer from depression and substance abuse at rates that are among the highest in the nation, suggests that the occupational stressors they endure are at least partly responsible. While it is beyond our scope to describe them all in detail, a summary account implicates a variety of environmental stressors in interaction with a number of predisposing individual characteristics.[21]

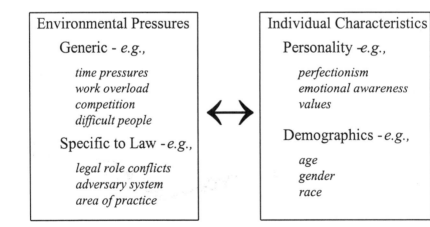

Some of the environmental stressors are generic and apply to a number of occupations besides law, whereas others are specifically indigenous to law. In addition, there are personality traits and demographic characteristics that make some lawyers more susceptible to stress. These factors do not act independently, but are tied together in an intricate web. Depending on your analytical starting point, each of them is sometimes the cause and sometimes the effect.

As documented in the preceding chapter, among the primary complaints that lawyers cite as contributing to their stress are time pressures, work overload, and inadequate time for themselves and their families. Simple statistics as well as descriptive accounts suggest that many legal workplaces are like blue collar sweat shops.[22] The typical lawyer is expected to log a minimum of 1800 billable hours per year; many lawyers are expected to far exceed this figure. An 1800 hour minimum translates into almost 7 hours per day, 5 days per week, 52 weeks a year. Since this does not include, eating, socializing, going to meetings, reading mail, seeking new clients, etc., it has been estimated that to bill 7 hours one must work 9-12 hours. Thus, it is common for lawyers to take work home, to work on weekends, and to not take their allotted vacation or holiday time.

As the number of lawyers climbs higher and higher, some blame their pressures on competition. Indeed, the growth in the number of attorneys in the U.S. has been geometric.[23] In 1950 there were 200,000 lawyers in the U.S., or one lawyer for every 750 people. The number of lawyers in this country grew to 280,000 by 1970, to over 400,000 by 1980, and to over 780,000 by 1992. It is estimated that there will be 1 million lawyers by the year 2000, or one lawyer for every 300 people in the U.S.

Other factors that have contributed to greater competition include slower economic growth in the general economy, corporate downsizing, and tort reform. These and other developments have caused lower morale, job insecurity and less loyalty. In summary, lawyers as well as many other professional groups in this country have found that during the 1980s and 1990s, making a living has been become more difficult.

Some lawyers attribute their stress to less than ideal work-site atmospheres. They complain about political intrigue and backbiting, disrespect and incivility from superiors and adversaries, poor clerical and paralegal assistance, and unfair promotion procedures. Others point to the fact that many law firms have such a strong profit motive that they lack many human values. These attorneys often feel like commodities that can be used, discarded, and easily replaced. It is generally known that our adversarial legal system may be partly to blame for promoting a Machiavellian environment, in which aggression, selfishness, hostility, suspiciousness, and cynicism are widespread. This causes a number of distressful effects, including generalized irritability and anxiety.

Another set of concerns that lawyers experience involves conflict and ambiguity about their roles in society. Some lawyers report feeling conflicted between their roles as officers of the court and as advocates for their clients. Sometimes they feel the tremendous weight that comes with being responsible for solving other people's problems within a context where mistakes are very costly. At other times they report feeling guilty about the fact that they are often forced to hurt people, some of whom have already undergone tragic ordeals. These issues also underlie the antipathy that the general public feels for lawyers, which is itself another source of stress. In addition, too many lawyers report that they lack a feeling of making a real contribution to society.

Of course, not all areas of law or types of practice are equally stressful. Generally, the private practice environment tends to be more stressful than the corporate or government setting. One exception to this rule is the public defender's role, a government position that tends to very stressful. Litigators report more stress than other colleagues. Certain areas of practice, such as family and criminal law also tend to be particularly stressful. Three underlying factors appear to make a difference: workload, time pressures, and amount of conflict.

In addition to the external stressors, there are individual traits that must be entered into the formula as well. For example, perfectionism is a common personality trait among lawyers that makes them more susceptible to stress. Perfectionistic people live by the following rules: "I must do a perfect job or I will fail. I need to be in total control. Details are extremely important." While some perfectionism is necessary in the practice of law, when taken too far it creates an enormous amount of distress. Since the true probability of everything going according to plan is close to zero, perfectionists tend to be perpetually disappointed.

Another common trait among lawyers that causes stress is that they tend to be exceedingly analytical "thinkers." In fact, a recent national study of over 1200 lawyers revealed that 77% of them prefer to make decisions on the basis of emotionally detached logical analysis. [24] These data suggest that a significant number of lawyers do not fully appreciate the positive role that emotions can play in human cognition. Thus, they tend to lack the ability to deal with their own emotions in the healthiest of ways, and tend to be insensitive to the feelings of others.

It is a fact of life that our adversarial legal system stimulates feelings of hostility, cynicism, aggression, fear and low self-esteem. Lawyers who are not adept at handling such emotions or who have a predisposition for experiencing them, will be more likely to feel stress. Similarly, because legal outcomes are not always "just," lawyers who are not skilled at handling their emotions may feel either too disappointed or too detached. Either extreme reduces job satisfaction and personal fulfillment.

Another factor that has been partly blamed for the stress lawyers experience is the ascendancy of materialistic values. A number of legal scholars[25] nostalgically recall a time when law was more of a profession and less of a business. Their view is that not too long ago lawyers were much more devoted to the rule of law and to such principles as integrity, commitment, and good will. They were less focused on economic self-interest, felt more in control of their lives, had a greater sense of contributing to society, and were more highly respected by others.

Finally, such demographic characteristics as race, age and gender also have been shown to be risk factors for stress among lawyers. Members of minority groups and women[26] in the law complain about job discrimination. Female attorneys express higher rates of job dissatisfaction due to sexual harassment. Younger and female lawyers also experience more conflicts about balancing work with family obligations.

THE PLIGHT OF YOUNG AND FEMALE ATTORNEYS

"At the end of your life, you will never regret not having passed one more test, not winning one more verdict or not closing one more deal. You will regret time not spent with a husband, a friend, a child or a parent. "   *Barbara Bush*

Several surveys of American attorneys have demonstrated that an excessive number of young attorneys and female attorneys are dissatisfied with their jobs. For example, a national ABA survey[27] conducted in 1984 found that although 15% of all respondents expressed significant job dissatisfaction, women did so at almost twice that rate (29%). A follow-up national survey[28] in 1990 found that whereas 19% of all attorneys reported being generally dissatisfied with their jobs, a much more dramatic picture emerged when the sample was broken down by age and gender. Among male attorneys who had graduated from law school after 1967 and were currently in private practice, 28% reported being generally dissatisfied with their jobs. As many as 41% of their female cohorts reported general dissatisfaction with their jobs.

Reportedly, what young or female lawyers find most troublesome about law is the amount of time they spend working at the expense of all other activities.[29] In a 1995 survey[30] conducted by the ABA Young Lawyers Division, 30% of ABA members who were under the age of 36 or admitted into practice for less than 3 years were dissatisfied with the allocation of time between their work and personal lives. This complaint was more prevalent among lawyers working for large firms. Compared to 23% of young lawyers in 1-2 person firms, over 62% of young lawyers in 150+ person firms expressed unhappiness about their inability to live a balanced life.

In a study conducted by the North Carolina Bar Association,[31] 43% of the close to 2600 attorneys surveyed in that state, reported that "the demands of their work do not allow them to have a satisfying non-work life (i.e., personal, family, social, civic)." Of those who were divorced or separated, 36% blamed the failure of their marriages partly on the pressures of their jobs. Among lawyers who had never been married, 46% said that the pressures of their jobs were partly to blame for that as well. A consistent finding throughout the North Carolina data is that younger and female lawyers were significantly more dissatisfied with the quality and quantity of their leisure time than older and male attorneys.

Even though young and female attorneys are concerned about a variety of problems with the practice of law, it is not surprising that "work overdose" is their most frequent complaint. Young attorneys (both males and females) are in the stages of life where they need more personal time to find a mate and get married or to spend with their newly formed families. Too often, they find that they can't do that and get ahead in law at the same time.

Female attorneys, regardless of their age, face a similar plight. Although our society has come a long way in terms of women's rights, it is still more socially acceptable (though not healthy) for men to neglect their families. Women are expected to be the primary caretakers of children at all ages, as well as elderly parents. In general, law is simply not a "family friendly" profession. This, plus the fact that female attorneys tend to be more in touch with their emotions[32] than their male cohorts, creates more internal turmoil regarding their time allocations.

THE WORKAHOLIC LAWYER

The single most frequent complaint about the practice of law is the "hours."[33] Indeed, the great majority of lawyers work more than the national standard of 40 hours per week. They commonly take work home after an exhausting day, come in to their offices on weekends, fail to take their full vacations, and often operate in a crisis mode. For some (too many) lawyers, work pervades everything. Even what seems to be personal time (e.g., watching a movie) is often secretly spent thinking about work.

"Workaholism" does have obvious benefits, but these come at a price.[34] Workaholics tend to develop headaches, sleep disturbances, high blood pressure, and other more serious illnesses. They are prone to acquire various food, alcohol and drug addictions. In addition, they have difficulty establishing or maintaining close personal relationships, and they have higher divorce and failed parenting rates. Finally, it is not unusual for them to experience depression, anxiety, and even more serious emotional illnesses --- and eventually to "burn out."

The stress typically associated with the practice of law makes workaholic lifestyles even more risky. Lawyers constantly take on the weight of other people's problems. They commonly deal with clients and adversaries who are emotionally strained and at their worst. And, of course, attorneys are often embroiled in conflict and involved with hostile opponents. Law professors also may work long hours but, because they do not experience the same stress as practitioners, are less likely to feel the deleterious effects.

From a health perspective, all of this suggests that many lawyers need to work less than the average number of hours, not more. So, why are so many of them working so many hours? Who or what is to blame?

Accusing senior partners of being too demanding is easy, but this explanation is probably too simplistic. Although many senior partners do indeed pay little attention to the personal human needs of their associates, they are usually even worse at taking care of their own. Also, some of the most workaholic law firms of all are solo practices. Similarly, workaholism cannot be totally blamed on a current recession or on increased competition; long hours is a way of life for many lawyers during prosperous times as well.

The truth is, workaholism among lawyers has a number of intertwined root causes that are psychological in nature. Although the following are neither exhaustive nor universally applicable, they apply to a considerable number of attorneys.

JUSTIFIABLE PARANOIA

One root cause of workaholism is in the very nature of our adversarial legal system, which requires many lawyers to adopt a dog-eat-dog world view. Within this environment, it is realistic for lawyers to suspect that people have ulterior motives, that it is safer to be secretive, that others will seize every opportunity to take advantage, and that manipulation and selfishness is widespread. In such an adversarial context, thinking this way is necessary for victorious survival and reflects nothing more than professional competence.

When mentally ill patients have "unwarranted" suspicions about the actions of other people, it is called "paranoid ideation." The most common effects of paranoid thinking include generalized irritability, anxiety, and fear, along with physical symptoms like "butterflies in the stomach" and insomnia. These emotions drive paranoid people to invest enormous amounts of energy into thinking of ways to avoid anticipated harm.

Although the suspiciousness that lawyers experience is often justified and cannot itself be clinically classified as "paranoia", it does have similar ill effects. At the very least, performance anxieties are likely to force many lawyers into workaholic behavior and thought patterns. In addition, since suspicious ideation is difficult to turn off and on at will, it is likely to spill into and damage their relationships with associates, friends, and family members. In turn, this causes feelings of isolation, loneliness, and depersonalization.

The best advice for people who are forced to work in a psychologically antagonistic environment is to limit exposure to it. Workaholic schedules should be minimized and more time should be spent in activities with family and friends, so that humanistic feelings can be rekindled. Given all of the other forces that drive workaholic attorneys, however, this advice is easier given than followed.

PERFECTIONISTIC THINKING

Another cause of workaholism among lawyers is the fact that "law" is driven by rules, order and organization, and thus, requires logical thought, objective analysis, and close attention to details. Lawyers are regularly judged on their ability to apply these skills within a context where mistakes can be very costly. This raises performance anxiety and induces perfectionistic thinking, which in turn leads to an obsessive dedication to work.

On one hand, perfectionism drives people to achieve professional success and is reinforced through praise and recognition. On the other hand, the urge to be perfect can lead to indecision, procrastination, and excessive thoroughness. Thus, when taken to extremes, it actually inhibits productivity. In addition, since perfection cannot be fully achieved, striving for perfection can cause chronic discontent and low job satisfaction. In other words, it takes the fun out of work.

Those who enter the law with perfectionistic tendencies are particularly susceptible to having work take over their lives. Since there is always room for improvement, perfectionists have difficulty knowing when to let go of their work and stop researching, rewriting and preparing. At times, deadlines are their only salvation. Perfectionistic lawyers also tend to spread themselves too thin. That is, they anticipate (imagine) that events in the future will go more smoothly (perfectly) than they have in the past and, as a result, tend to take on more work than they can handle.

This type of thinking also spills into lawyers' personal lives in a number of ways. Being excessively in control at work tends to choke off spontaneity everywhere else. Perfectionists are often viewed by others as people who do not know how to relax or have fun. They also tend to be critical and demanding. These qualities often have disastrous consequences for their relationships with spouses, children, and friends. Unfortunately, workaholic perfectionists sometimes compensate for their failures at home by devoting even more time to work.

INSATIABLE DESIRE FOR SUCCESS

Many lawyers, as well as others in our society, become workaholics because they are driven by an insatiable desire to achieve an ever increasing level of professional and financial success. Such individuals make the mistake of believing that success has a satiation point, and that it is possible to get there more quickly by "temporarily" sacrificing one's personal life. For example, some may say, "As soon as I make partner, I'll pay attention to my other needs." Since past professional goals are constantly replaced by new ones, other needs are in fact permanently deferred.

These lawyers seldom enjoy their professional and financial success; they live in the future, not in the present. No level of achievement is savored for very long before it is interrupted by the pressures of newly set ambitions. Success is elusive in that it is perpetually anticipated rather than experienced. Happiness is always foreseen, but seldom felt.

In addition to a mistaken belief that professional or financial success has a satiation point, these attorneys often are out of touch with the psychological needs they are really trying to satisfy. That is, an uncontrolled drive to succeed is frequently related to a deeper need for security, love, esteem, power, or autonomy. For example, few people want a great deal of money per se; in many cases wealth represents a way of getting love and admiration. In reality, a more balanced personal life can achieve these psychological needs more effectively than workaholism. Sadly, this fact is rarely understood.

THE TYPE OF PRACTICE
ALSO MATTERS

To some extent, the stressors that affect lawyers are a product of the type of organization in which they work, the types of law they practice and the kinds of clients they represent. Approximately 75% of lawyers who have legal positions are in a private practice setting, whereas most of the rest are employed in corporate legal departments or in government agencies.[35] These settings range in size from one lawyer to several hundred. Since law regulates almost every type of human behavior, there are a variety of substantive areas in which lawyers develop special expertise, including: commercial, torts, tax, real estate, criminal, labor, matrimonial, patent, public interest, etc. All of these differences affect the types of stress lawyers experience.

For example, when compared to their peers in private practice, lawyers in corporate legal departments tend to complain more often about such problems as lack of opportunity for advancement and professional development, political intrigue and backbiting.[36] On the other hand, lawyers in private practice are much more likely to suffer the effects of not having enough time for themselves and their families, and of being under pressure to produce income.

Large private practice firms are more likely to place their attorneys under the pressure of greater billable hour requirements, more staff meetings and other administrative duties. The larger the firm, the more likely it is that its lawyers have to contend with office politics, power plays, and competition for advancement or the firm's resources. Unless their work climate is carefully and explicitly managed, larger law firms tend to have authoritarian, overly demanding and personally insensitive environments. Lawyers in the middle and lower levels of the hierarchy don't feel in control of their lives or careers.

In contrast, solo practitioners do have the advantages of being their own bosses. No one tells them what cases to take or how many hours to work, and they don't have to share their income with others. On the other hand, in addition to providing legal services, "solos" have to find time to create bills, pay bills, make purchasing decisions, market their practice, file and type. "Solos" take the risk of being totally responsible for their own decisions, and are exclusively in charge of the "complaint department." In addition, they have to deal with feelings of isolation and the fears that accompany slow business months.

Litigators of all stripes probably endure more stress than non-litigators. Their stress becomes especially acute when they go to trial.[37] Starting with the pretrial phase, litigators report various physical symptoms, including headaches, skin rashes, gastrointestinal ailments, and insomnia. Out of a fear of forgetting something, they spend endless hours preparing, only to be disappointed by inevitable postponements. Once the trial phase begins, the anticipatory anxiety diminishes but is replaced by physical exhaustion. Handling their clients' emotionalism and preparing for each day of trial can take up every available waking minute. Family and other obligations are often simply not attended to and create their own pressures. After the trial, there is the inescapable letdown and obsessive replaying of all questions that should have been asked and closing statements that should have been made.

Finally, substantive areas of specialization also contribute to stress. For example, family law is a particularly stressful type of practice,[38] in part because divorcing clients are often highly emotional and on their worst behavior. Since the couple's relationship often continues to unravel throughout the divorce action, family lawyers and their staff commonly operate in crisis mode. Feelings of hostility, guilt, fear and frustration are rampant. Clients who want to do rotten things to their spouses look for willing lawyers. Thus, part of the job often involves contending with S.O.B. lawyers. With half of the populace having experienced a divorce, announcing that you are a divorce lawyer at a cocktail party has its hazards as well.

While it is beyond my scope to describe them all, each substantive area of practice has its stressors. Lawyers who shuffle commercial paper all day sometimes complain of tedium and tend to lack a sense of contributing to the social good. Criminal lawyers have to frequently endure the stress of witnessing the most evil aspects of human nature. Those who specialize in the emerging area of elder law often have to deal with family tragedies that come at the end of life. As advocates, lawyers cannot help but be touched by the problems of their clients.

SECTION III

SOLUTIONS: AN OVERVIEW OF STRESS MANAGEMENT TECHNIQUES

The best way out is always through.
                                    Robert Frost

The worst cynicism: a belief in luck.
                                    Joyce Carol Oates

WHAT IS STRESS?

Although law is a particularly stressful profession, it certainly is not unique. From prehistoric times, human beings have experienced occupational stress. In recent years, stress has been the subject of wide ranging scientific study. Since the findings of such studies apply to all persons, it is useful to learn a few facts about stress in general.

THE ELEMENTS OF STRESS

The human experience we call "stress" can be viewed as being composed of the following sequence of elements:[39]

Stimulus > Thought > Emotion > Behavior

For example, consider what happens when you see a car coming toward you in your lane of traffic. Your initial reaction is to perceptually or mentally appraise the situation. At a speed so fast that you may not be totally conscious of it, you think to yourself, " That passing car may not have enough time to get back into its lane. I'm in danger and I have to avoid it."

These thoughts trigger several internal bodily responses. Breathing gets faster, digestion slows down, heart rate and blood pressure go up, perspiration increases, and your total being becomes focused on the car that is coming toward you. Your thoughts combined with your internal bodily reactions create an emotion called fear. Then, your body goes into external action and you maneuver your car in a way that avoids a collision. Of course, this same car scene can also result in negative consequences when the fear created is so great that it causes panic, which in turn reduces your ability to act constructively.

Understanding how the elements of a stress response are interconnected gives us the ability to control our reactions. One way to control stress is simply to interrupt its stream of elements. For example, it is obvious that if the stimulus is interrupted or changed, the rest of the stress experience will be different. Note, however, that only the first element of the stress sequence occurs outside of us.[40] The other elements occur from within. Thus, another way to control stress is to interrupt or change our own thoughts, emotions, and behaviors. Indeed, several of the upcoming chapters in this book focus on how to do this.

STRESS IS HEALTHY
DISTRESS IS NOT

Certain forms of stress are inevitable and necessary to a healthy, productive, and happy life. Some of the stressors in our lives energize our positive emotions and motivate us to get up in the morning, solve problems, and be creative. Thus, getting rid of all stress is both a naive and harmful goal.

This point was illustrated to me in a cartoon I saw somewhere but cannot cite, depicting a street scene of a homeless beggar, who was once a successful lawyer, and his well dressed psychotherapist. Upon recognizing the therapist, the beggar runs after him and calls out: "Doc, doc! Don't you recognize me? You advised me to take it easy and let my practice take care of itself!"

Indeed, attempting to reduce all stress in life often is equivalent to running away from it all, which is not a formula for success. Your focus should be on reducing a destructive form of stress called distress. This form of stress is characterized by negative emotions such as fear, anxiety, shame, guilt, and anger. When such emotions are chronic and strong, they tend to destroy our ability to enjoy life, stay healthy, and work productively.

Some people assume that an ability to endure distress is a sign of strong character or courage. I believe that passive endurance of distress is more often a sign of bad judgment and fear of change. My objective is to help you overcome life's harmful challenges, not just endure them. This takes real guts and ingenuity.

MYTH: PSYCHOLOGICAL AND PHYSICAL STRESS ARE SEPARATE

For every thought and emotion we experience, there is a corresponding biochemical correlate. Thus, thoughts and emotions are both physiological and psychological. They are reflections of the same phenomenon, measured from different levels of analysis.[41] When we experience psychological distress two things happen concurrently: we feel negative emotions and undergo internal bodily changes.

It should not be surprising that when harm is done in the psychological realm, harm is done in the physical realm as well. For example, recent studies have shown that diseases associated with the blood circulatory system as well as the immune system can be influenced by our thoughts and emotions.[42] These findings suggest that stress management is much more than just a way to achieve psychological health. It is something you do to maintain both your mental and physical health, for they are interrelated.

THE BASIC PRINCIPLES OF STRESS MANAGEMENT

Turning to what you can do about stress, let me begin by bringing the principles of stress management down to the simplest of terms. From time immemorial, threats of all kinds have left both animals and humans with only three options: *surrender, flee, or fight.* Although we may use different descriptors today, the choices we face in reacting to the stressful events of our modern society are still remarkably similar.

THE SURRENDER OPTION

A current form of surrender is when you passively accept your stressful circumstances as inevitable and simply suffer the consequences. Of course some acts of endurance over stress are courageous, but many are not. I am referring to people who accept their stressors when they can do something about them. Usually, the emotions that drive such behaviors are fear and helplessness. In turn, these emotions often result in anxiety disorders and clinical depression.[43]

Interestingly, when you cope with psychological stress in a passive-depressive manner, a type of surrender also occurs at the biochemical level. Your brain adapts to prolonged distress by accepting it as normal and begins to suppress the activity of your immune system, which in turn makes you more susceptible to invading foreign cells. Preliminary evidence suggests that people in chronic passive distress or depression have higher rates of cancer.[44] In addition, it is a well established fact that coronary disease can be partly caused by chronic distress and depression.[45] For all of these reasons, surrender is not a good option.

THE FLIGHT OPTION

The underlying strategy of the flight option is to reduce stress by removing yourself from its sources. You can remove yourself from or avoid the causes of your stress either externally or internally. Quitting your job, being assigned to a new department, working fewer hours, and taking a vacation or a sabbatical are examples of how we remove ourselves from stressful activities externally. Some of these tactics rejuvenate our ability to endure stress in the future (e.g., sabbatical).

Daydreaming is one way that we remove ourselves from stressful situations internally, without ever physically leaving our offices. The most effective way to do this is through formal *relaxation techniques* that involve breathing exercises, muscle relaxation, and mental imagery (e.g., meditation, Yoga). These techniques work because they allow you to focus your mind on something pleasant and different. They also have positive biochemical effects, such as reducing blood pressure.[46]

I have categorized relaxation techniques under the flight option because their immediate effect is only temporary. It should be mentioned, however, that people who do these exercises on a regular basis also experience long term attitudinal transformations. For this reason, an argument could be made for categorizing relaxation techniques under the fight option below.

THE FIGHT OPTION

Another way to reduce stress is to confront its sources and alter them. You can do this externally by improving your *work environment*. Or, you can do this internally by acting on either your body or your mind in some way. *Nutrition and exercise* are physical ways to reduce your stress internally. Controlling your *thoughts and emotions* is the psychological way to reduce your stress internally.

WHICH OPTION IS BETTER?

Most people gravitate naturally toward the flight option. In the short run, it is generally easier to avoid rather than confront a problem. However, avoidance is seldom effective in the long run. Its results are only temporary, as in the case of a vacation, or very costly, as in the case of a career change. (Obviously, I am all for lawyers taking their vacations, and do favor career changes in some instances.) Although confronting problems head on is the most difficult option, it does lead to more permanent solutions.

THE WORK ENVIRONMENT

Most stress management consultants advise lawyers on how to increase their resistance to environmental stressors and ignore the possibility that those stressors themselves can be reduced in the first place. On the other hand, when consultants do suggest the latter possibility, most lawyers take a passive stance of resignation regarding their own working conditions and reject the suggested improvements as naive and idealistic. What is truly unrealistic is the idea that lawyers can overcome all of the stressors in today's legal workplaces on their own, without the aid of environmental improvements.

Their passive attitude does not conform with the fact that, historically, lawyers have been in the forefront of helping other groups within our society achieve humane labor laws and standards. There is no reason why lawyers cannot apply those same talents toward reforming their own working conditions. Although most of this book is devoted to what individuals can do, without a group effort on the part of the legal community, law is doomed to remain a most stressful profession.

One place to start is at the law firm level. Indeed, a number of bar organizations have issued recommendations on how employment policies within law firms can be improved to make lawyers' lives less stressful.[47] They have endorsed alternative work schedules, flexible billable hour requirements, improved communication with associates and clients, greater training opportunities, and more mentoring. Law firms that run like white collar sweat shops in the name of fiscal intelligence are truly behind the times. Many of the most competitive world class corporations in the U.S. have found that helping their employees balance work with family life helps - not hurts - the bottom line; it increases loyalty and productivity.[48]

If law is to become less stressful, certain aspects of the legal system also need to be reformed. For example, if it is true that some of the stress lawyers experience results from the adversarial nature of our legal process, then it follows that alternative dispute resolution options should lead to less distress. Albeit for different reasons, many jurisdictions are experimenting with such reforms. In evaluating their efficacy, the Bar should consider how alternative dispute resolution methods affect lawyers' well-being.

The number and scope of interrogatories, depositions, motions and pleadings that are currently allowed in a single case is another possible area for reform. Streamlining these procedures may decrease the worst types of stress producing games that the system encourages. Ways in which courts schedule their cases also need to be reviewed and possibly reformed. Some scheduling procedures are either too unpredictable or do not allow enough advance notice, and cause lawyers much disruption. Another lament I have heard is the frequency with which judges ask for a brief on a Friday afternoon with a Monday morning deadline, never considering what this does to the attorneys' personal lives.

Ethical guidelines regulating the practice of law also may be in need of examination. For example, it has been reported that lawyers' multiple duties to represent clients and serve as officers of the court sometimes creates stress-producing role conflicts. Programs such as the American Inns of Court help lawyers grapple with such difficult ethical dilemmas in a supportive environment, but more needs to be done.

Finally, policies that regulate the education of lawyers also need to be examined. Teaching students to "think like a lawyer," often translates into an impersonal study of law. Perhaps law school curricula should devote some attention to the human aspects of practicing law. This could include courses on the very topics covered in this book.

RELAXATION TECHNIQUES

Imagine that it is two o'clock in the afternoon, the phone has been interrupting you all day, you have been insulted numerous times, and you just can't seem to concentrate on the brief that is due tomorrow morning. You don't have the time to ponder the meaning of it all. You need a quick method of calming down. Saying "relax" to yourself just does not do it. This is a good time to try relaxation exercises. They provide effective temporary relief of stress symptoms, such as negative thoughts and emotions, muscle tension, upset stomach, and high blood pressure.

In general, there are three types of relaxation exercises you can learn and use in various combinations:[49]

- Muscle Relaxation
- Breathing Exercises
- Mental Imagery

To understand how these techniques work, remember that the mind and body are not separate entities. Thus, whenever we experience stressful thoughts, there are concurrent physiological correlates such as muscle tension, faster breathing, higher blood pressure, etc. Conversely, whenever we feel the physical symptoms of distress, we are also more likely to have stressful thoughts.

Relaxation techniques are based on the idea that since mind and body are part of one unified whole, it is possible to affect the body through the mind and the mind through the body. With muscle relaxation and breathing exercises, one focuses primarily on the body, whereas with mental imagery the focus is on the mind. In each instance, however, the purpose is to interrupt the stress pattern at any level and thereby reduce stress in the whole organism.

A typical muscle relaxation exercise is one in which you find a comfortable place to sit and begin by concentrating on your muscular tensions. The idea is to focus your total attention on your body. Start either at the top or the bottom and progressively move to the other end. Then begin tensing and relaxing each muscle group. For example, wiggle and tighten the muscles in your feet and toes for a few seconds and then release them, noticing how it feels to relax. You might even repeat the word "relax" to yourself silently. Then, doing the same thing, progressively move up your body to the other muscle areas, such as those in your legs, hips, stomach, back, arms, shoulders, neck and head.

Another type of exercise, which you can use alone or in combination with the others, is breathing. Again, find a comfortable and quiet place to sit, close your eyes and begin breathing more deeply than usual. As you do this, chase all intruding thoughts away and concentrate on just your breathing. Listen to the sounds as if they were waves in the ocean. Feel the air bathing your lungs and imagine the extra cleansing your blood stream is getting.

Finally, you can try a variety of imagery exercises. Here the idea is to create relaxing images in your mind and experience the pleasure they bring. You might picture yourself on a sail boat, lying under a tree, or playing with your children. Use all of your senses in your images. For example, listen to the sounds of a summer wind and feel its warmth. Also, create interpretative verbal messages; silently comment on how peaceful it is or how much you love watching your children smile.

If you are reluctant to try relaxation techniques, you are not alone. Many lawyers feel awkward and silly trying them, and the mysticism that is sometimes attached to discussions about meditation does not help. Do not be put off by such connections. You really do not need to adopt a new religion or burn incense to benefit from relaxation exercises.

Some lawyers are reluctant to try relaxation exercises out of a puritanical belief that there is something wrong with relaxation. Others have a mistaken fear that relaxation will cause them to have less energy and make them lose their desire to work. In fact, relaxation exercises take just 10-20 minutes, and will make you more alert, more able to withstand long hours and more able to be productive.

Again, note that relaxation exercises can provide effective short term relief of distress or give you a refreshing recess during a hard working day. People who practice relaxation techniques on a regular basis also report long term benefits. To understand why, it is instructive to know that in order to get good at relaxation, you must learn to focus on the task of relaxing and not allow distractions such as noises or your own thoughts to interrupt you. This ability to "let go of things" is an important element of stress reduction in general. People who get good at it during their relaxation exercises maintain that attitude throughout the day. In this way, relaxation helps them develop a greater sense of calm and control over a variety of annoyances. In addition, it stimulates them to reexamine what is truly worth getting upset about in their lives.

My description of these techniques is introductory. Should you decide to read more comprehensive treatments of this topic, note that books by Herbert Benson, M.D., are highly respected and strongly recommended.[50] Among other excellent books on this subject is *The Relaxation & Stress Reduction Workbook*, written by Martha Davis, Elizabeth Eshelman and Mathew

McKay.[51] A series of companion audiotapes can be purchased through the same publisher.[52] Tapes make the practice of relaxation exercises much easier, by walking you through the necessary steps and providing soothing background music. Of course, there are many other good books[53] and tapes[54] on relaxation techniques at your local bookstore or library.

EXERCISE AND NUTRITION

The physical benefits of good nutrition and regular exercise are well known. They help prevent illness, increase life expectancy, and improve physical appearance. These effects also lift psychological well being. That is, people with good muscle tone, ideal weight, normal blood pressure, and fewer illnesses of all types are obviously less likely to worry about their appearance and physical health. In addition, proper nutrition and exercise actually change the chemistry of the brain. People who eat the right foods and exercise regularly report experiencing more positive moods, having higher psychic energy and mental concentration levels, getting more sleep, and feeling less muscle tension. In turn, this also increases their capacity to withstand the strains of the world around them.

Thus, if you want to reduce the stresses in your life, nutrition and exercise need to be part of your strategy. The first thing to do is arm yourself with reliable information. There are a number of good books available on these topics, but consider making the following ones a part of your library:

Covert Bailey, The Fit or Fat Target Diet (1984).

Covert Bailey, The New Fit or Fat (1991).

Kenneth Cooper, The Aerobics Program for Total Well Being: Exercise, Diet, Emotional Balance (1991)

Editors of Berkeley Wellness Letter,
The New Wellness Encyclopedia (1995)

Although most people would benefit from additional information about nutrition and exercise, there already is a great deal of awareness about these issues. For example, my seminar participants know that: "You are supposed to watch both the quantity and quality of the foods you eat, and do physical exercises on a regular basis." When I press them for specifics, they all know about the hazards of fats, sugars, salt, cholesterol, too many calories, etc. They all know that you are supposed to do aerobic exercises at least three times per week for at least 20-30 minutes. Some of them are capable of going into great detail about these matters. I then ask how many of them actually follow their own advice. At this point, very few hands go up and there is nervous laughter.

My last question serves to make a crucial point. When it comes to nutrition and exercise, as well as many other things in life, most of us know what to do but cannot seem to get ourselves to do it. This is the reason that weight loss and exercise services and products comprise a multi-billion dollar industry. It feeds on our illusion that if we invest in one more diet book, piece of exercise equipment, or health club membership, we will finally do the right things. Soon, however, our tried and tested excuses take over: "I'm too busy. It's too expensive. It's not fun." Only after a heart attack or another illness do some of us become more disciplined.

The underlying problem with doing the right thing regarding nutrition and exercise is that the pain comes before the gain. When we eat that extra dessert or skip our exercise, just the opposite occurs; pleasure precedes the costs. It is in our biological nature to be strongly drawn to the latter arrangement. This is one reason why addictive behaviors, such as problem drinking, are so difficult to break.

Allow me to introduce you to three principles that you can use to overcome the strong pull of negative behaviors over positive ones. The examples I present are intended only to illustrate the general principles, and do not represent an exhaustive list of the concrete steps you can take. My purpose is to encourage you to embed the general principles firmly in your mind and then find multiple ways of applying them to your particular situation. (Note that there is evidence to suggest that our diet and physical activity levels are partly regulated by genetic predispositions. While we cannot change our genetic predispostions, we can modulate them by learning to think, feel and act in certain ways.)

One thing you can do to overcome a strong desire to eat poorly or refrain from exercise is to get into the habit of mentally accentuating the costs of such behaviors. For example, whenever you find yourself automatically thinking that you don't have the time to exercise, interrupt yourself and rephrase your sentences. Say something like the following to yourself: "I don't have the time to prolong my life or reduce my chances of getting seriously ill. These are just not among my priorities. Billing my clients for a few extra hours is much more important." Since your brain is programmed to avoid pain, accentuating the costs of not doing the right thing will trigger fear in you, which in turn will eventually motivate you to behave differently.

Another thing to do is make appropriate eating and exercise behaviors as pleasurable and painless as possible. Accept the fact that human beings are hedonistic animals and that you are no exception. Watch television, listen to music videos, or do whatever else is necessary to make your regular exercise routine pleasurable. If you are a walker, get a significant other to do it with you. You will spend quality time together, while getting a good workout. When you go out to dinner with your family, order one dessert for the whole table and plenty of forks and spoons. It will not feel like you are depriving yourself of anything. You will get a taste of the sweet stuff, enjoy the experience of sharing, and model appropriate behaviors to your children.

Finally, if you truly want to get control of your nutrition and exercise program, create external stimuli that elicit positive behaviors. You can spend countless hours philosophizing about free will, but if you really want to get control of yourself, accept the fact that subtle environmental cues play a powerful role in directing your behaviors. For example, there is only one way to stop me from eventually eating that dark semi-sweet chocolate that I love so much: leave it at the store. When making a choice between placing your exercise equipment in your basement or in your bedroom, choose the latter. You will be much more likely to use it in the comfort of your bedroom, especially when it stares at you each morning and cries out: "Use me!"

THOUGHTS AND EMOTIONS

Consider a situation in which two associates have scheduled several meetings with an attorney from another firm to finalize a deal for their respective clients. Each time, the lawyer for the other side is late in arriving. One associate concludes that the late comer must not have much respect for their time. This thought leads him to feel hurt and angry, and to be somewhat cool and hostile at the meetings.

In contrast, his colleague concludes that this is a guy who is constantly trying to squeeze more out of a day than is possible. Her thoughts also lead to mild annoyance, but not anger. More importantly, she feels some apprehension about the possibility that this colleague may cut corners and do careless work. As a result, she decides to be friendly at the meetings, but to be very cautious and proof read all materials very closely.

How can the same situation create such different reactions? It occurs because humans are not automatons who respond in purely mechanical ways. Our various physiological constitutions and learning experiences result in a unique combination of personality traits - ways of thinking, feeling, and behaving. In turn, our personalities have a great deal to do with how we respond to the world around us.

Everything we perceive and all of our mental processes are a function of both objective reality and subjective interpretation, which is both active and amenable to change. This point can be demonstrated very simply by looking at the following cube:

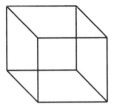

There are two ways to view it. One way is to perceive the front panel of the cube facing down and to the right. The other way is to see the front panel facing up and to the left:

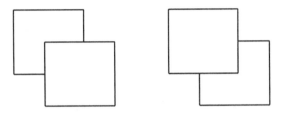

Now look at the full cube above and try to shift views at will. Your ability to do this demonstrates the fact that although the external stimuli remain the same, human perception is active, not passive. We have the ability to see things from different points of view at will. Most lawyers already know this to be true and can point to many instances of it in their work. A good example is how jurors interpret the so called "facts" of a case. These same lawyers, however, have a much more difficult time being aware of how their own perceptions affect their lives.

In the next two sections, I am going to ask you to willingly shift your points of view in matters that cause you distress. The strategy involves confronting your own psyche and considering how alternative interpretations to the same situations and events can have a profound effect on your emotions and behaviors. The strategies that I cover are easy to explain, but difficult to effectuate. This is why some people do seek professional help. Yet, when we study people who achieve contentment without the aid of professionals, we find that they use the same tactics.[55] Thus, this is something that you can learn on your own.

SECTION IV

IMPROVE

YOUR

THINKING

There is nothing either good or bad, but thinking makes it so.

William Shakespeare

The greatest discovery of my generation is that human beings can alter their lives by altering their attitudes of mind.

William James

UNDERSTAND, EVALUATE
AND IMPROVE

Let us say that a judge criticizes you in open court, in front of your colleagues, your client and the jury. Such an event might stimulate you to think to yourself: "This is making me look bad! I should have been better prepared! I'm going to lose this case! The judge really didn't have to treat me this way!" Thoughts like these evoke several negative emotions, including embarrassment, fear, guilt and anger. The bodily reactions that are part of these emotions jolt you into behaving differently.

Notice that only the first element of the experience, the judge's remarks, happens outside of you. The rest of it occurs from within, where your individuality exerts control. Thus, the same external events can create a variety of internal reactions in different people or in the same people at different times. For example, although the initial negative reactions to a critical judge may be universal, how long they persist depends on you. You may continue to say to yourself, "I am going to lose this case and the respect of everyone in the courtroom!" On the other hand, you may switch gears and say to yourself, "What is it that the judge wants me to do and how can I do it?"

The choice you make has significant consequences. If your thoughts continue to focus solely on the problem and its repercussions, what you fear may indeed occur and your level of distress will increase. On the other hand, if your reasoning shifts and you begin thinking about solutions to the problem, positive results are more likely to follow and your level of distress will diminish.

What causes some people to concentrate on problems and others on solutions? In one word, the answer is "habits." As if to disagree, some people would say that personality is the determining factor. The word "personality," however, is nothing more than a label we attach to a set of habitual ways of thinking, feeling and acting. For example, someone with a perfectionistic personality is a person with a habit of thinking that everything they do must be perfect.

From an evolutionary perspective, your ability to develop habits has adaptive value. Habits allow you to respond to events automatically, and alleviate the need to reanalyze each situation as if it is a new experience. Imagine what life would be like if you could not rely on your automatic pilot to do such things as walk up a staircase or stop a car at a red light. As we all know, however, the downside is that some of the habits we develop are not adaptive. More on point, certain maladaptive mental and emotional habits make stressful situations worse rather than better.

Obviously, the thing to do is to unlearn such habits and replace them with more adaptive ones. After years of repetition, however, certain habitual thoughts, emotions, and behaviors become so deeply ingrained that they feel permanent. Nevertheless, this is only an illusion since no learned response is etched in stone. You do have the power to change.

To accomplish this goal, you need to get into the habit of taking three basic steps. First, become aware of and *understand* your stress reactions. Then, *evaluate* which of your habitual reactions are maladaptive. Finally, *improve* matters by replacing your maladaptive reactions with beneficial ones.

FIRST, UNDERSTAND YOUR STRESS REACTIONS

Your typical stress reactions are likely to be so automatic and to occur so quickly that you may not even be aware of them.

The road to improvement starts with slowing your reactions down to the point where you do become fully aware of them. Only then will you be able to turn off the automatic pilot and steer yourself in new directions.

The best way to become aware of the specific stimuli, thoughts, emotions, and behaviors that contribute to your distress is to keep a daily log of them for about two weeks. Simply divide a blank sheet of paper into four columns: stimuli, thoughts, emotions and behaviors. If you prefer, make copies of and use the top portion of the sample form provided at the end of this chapter. Then, choose one or two stress-producing events per day and record them as you would in a diary. The only difference is that this log requires you to dissect each experience down to its elements.

For example, suppose an associate upsets you by turning in a legal brief that does not meet your expectations. To fully understand your reactions, you would record the fact that you received such a brief in the first column. In the second column you would record thoughts such as: "This is unacceptable. You are incompetent. I need to do this myself." The resulting emotions like anger and fear of failure, would get entered in the third column. Finally, in the last column you would write the fact that you expressed your hostility toward your associate and began rewriting the brief yourself.

The first and last columns may be easier to complete than the two in the middle. Generally, it is easy to identify the external events that triggered your distress and your outward reactions to them. (An exception to this is that sometimes your own thoughts are the triggering events, and not anything in the environment.) Identifying the thoughts and emotions that occur in between will probably be more difficult. However, once you work through the initial difficulties and are able to record your thoughts and emotions a few dozen times, you will discover that the same limited number of themes will occur over and over again. At this point they will become easier to recognize, less automatic, and more conscious.

Recording your stress reactions a number of times should make you increasingly mindful of several facts. First, what underlies most distress are one or more negative emotions such as anger, guilt or fear. Emotions ultimately determine your external behaviors. So, whenever you are confused about your own motives, just pay attention to and identify your emotions.

What I hope you become most aware of, however, is the linkage that exists between your thoughts and emotions. As a matter of fact, my primary purpose in asking you to do this exercise is to make you conscious of the fact that your distressful emotions are triggered by your own negative thoughts. For example, there is no way that you can feel angry without first thinking, either consciously or unconsciously, that someone has done or is doing something objectionable. Becoming fully aware of how your negative thoughts cause your distressful emotions is not all you have to do to bring your stress under control, but it is a very significant step.

THEN, EVALUATE AND IMPROVE YOUR DYSFUNCTIONAL THINKING HABITS

The next thing you will need to realize is that many of your negative thinking patterns are the products of years of repetition and that they get activated without much conscious effort on your part. What makes them particularly destructive is that they occur automatically, regardless of whether they are inappropriate and dysfunctional.

To improve the way you typically react to things, you will need to break through your own conditioning by repeatedly *interrupting* its automatic flow. The way to do that is to constantly flesh out your stress-producing thoughts and bring them into full consciousness.

In addition to interrupting your automatic thoughts, *challenge* them and force yourself to prove their validity. Since people differ drastically in how they perceive similar events, ask yourself how others might view your situation and why. Consider all alternative interpretations and *evaluate* their validity. When warranted, consider *replacing* your initial thoughts and emotions with more adaptive ones

Finally, if you are still left with a problem, ask future oriented questions such as, "What can/will I do about this?" In other words, shift your focus away from simply repeating your problems and try to *generate solutions* to them. Then, imagine the emotions and behaviors that a solution-oriented line of reasoning will stimulate.

Allow me to illustrate this technique by way of a simple example. Suppose you get stuck with an unexpected amount of additional work and observe yourself thinking: "How will I ever find the time to handle all of these cases? I can't readjust my calendar. I will have to work this weekend and disappoint the kids again. What can I do?" Chances are that as soon as you begin thinking this way, certain emotions will get evoked, such as fear of failure, guilt and anger. You may find yourself unable to concentrate or work as efficiently as usual, and you may become more irritable with others.

"What can you do?" First, break your full reaction down to its elements as described above. Then, begin to question your automatic thought patterns. You might say to yourself: "Wait a minute! These are my automatic thoughts. That doesn't make them automatically right. When I say, 'How will I find the time?,' I am making an automatic judgment that there is no better solution to my problem than to work through the weekend. In addition, I am automatically predicting that if I make adjustments to my calendar, terrible things will happen."

In continuing your internal dialogue, consider such thoughts as: "Suppose I reverse my current thinking. Let me assume the possibility that there is a solution to my problem and that others might not think less of me if I adjust my calendar appropriately. Instead of asking the question in a rhetorical way, let me ask it again as a real question: 'How can I find the time to do all of this, without sacrificing my personal life?' One thing I can do is call one of these clients and ask if a short delay would ...." As you begin to explore various solutions to your problem in a creative and open ended way, you will notice your emotions and behaviors begin to change for the better.

At the end of this chapter there is a daily log that you can use to practice the technique just described. The top row asks you to simply become aware of the stimuli, the thoughts, the emotions and the behaviors that together define your stressful experience. The bottom row asks you to evaluate your thoughts and, if they are dysfunctional, to consider alternative ones.

It is best to do this exercise on paper at least a few times, just to fully comprehend the steps that are involved. As unnatural as it may seem, recording your internal dialogue on paper will have a strong positive effect on you. If you find yourself too reluctant to try the exercise on paper, don't give up on the entire approach. Just do as much of the exercise as you can in your mind. Particularly good times to practice the exercise in your mind are while you are taking a shower or driving a car. If you do it often enough, the exercise will become easier and easier. Eventually, it will become a natural part of the way you think. Your old negative thought patterns will simply dissipate.

The process I have described is effective, but difficult to do. Since it involves changing a part of your personality, it could be one of the most difficult tasks you will ever undertake. Do not expect quick results and you will not be disappointed. Do not give it up prematurely, saying to yourself, "I'll do this later, when I have more time." Ask yourself, "What are the chances of that happening?"

I wish I could recommend an easier solution, but if dysfunctional thinking is your problem, then there is no better way. Real change takes strength and courage, and requires you to break through much emotional resistance. On the positive side, however, courageous acts build self-esteem and lead to many other positive outcomes. Thus, even though what I am proposing is difficult, I offer it as something that is both doable and worthwhile.

The next several chapters are designed to help you carry out the details of this technique. Nevertheless, if you continue to experience high levels of distress or are unable to effectuate these proposed methods, you may want to consider the help of a mental health professional. If you decide to seek such help, note that my approach is based on a technique known as cognitive or rational-emotive psychotherapy. Because the vast majority of lawyers place great value on their rational and analytical skills, I have found that this approach is a natural match.

DAILY LOG OF STRESS REACTIONS & SOLUTIONS

WHAT HAPPENED? IDENTIFY EVENTS, SITUATIONS, OR THOUGHTS THAT STIMULATED STRESS.	IDENTIFY NEGATIVE THOUGHTS: SPECIFIC PERCEPTIONS & GENERAL RULES (e.g., "I am a failure.").	LABEL THE EMOTIONS YOUR THOUGHTS CREATED (e.g., Angry, Afraid, Guilty, Sad, Hurt, Suspicious, Jealous)	RESULTING BEHAVIORS: (e.g., Yelled, Withdrew, Couldn't Work, Complained)
IDENTIFY DISTORTED PERCEPTIONS & DYSFUNCTIONAL RULES. CONSIDER ALTERNATIVES. ASK SOLUTION/FUTURE ORIENTED QUESTIONS (e.g., "What can I do about this?").	PREDICT/DESCRIBE YOUR EMOTIONS UNDER A REVISED LINE OF REASONING.	PREDICT/DESCRIBE YOUR BEHAVIORS UNDER A REVISED LINE OF REASONING	

HOW TO ELIMINATE DYSFUNCTIONAL THINKING

To improve the way you react to stressful situations both emotionally and behaviorally, you need to replace certain habitual negative patterns of thinking with more adaptive ones. As discussed earlier, to accomplish this you must first *understand* that your stress reactions are composed of four elements: stimuli, thoughts, emotions and behaviors. In addition, you need to realize that distressful emotions are usually preceded by negative thoughts. Once you recognize the thoughts that underlie your emotional distress, you need to *evaluate* their validity and where indicated *improve* them. Since this task is complicated and difficult to implement, allow me to break it down into smaller steps and explain each of them in simple terms.

STEP 1:
ADOPT AN INVESTIGATIVE ATTITUDE

Your very first step is to adopt an investigative attitude in which you assume nothing about the validity of your stress producing thoughts. This is difficult to do because your thoughts are likely to be so automatic that they seem indisputable. You probably act as if the mere fact that they come to mind makes them true. Can you imagine acting this way when you develop legal arguments? Yet, when it comes to personal matters, this is the kind of illogic that makes some people accept a great deal of their own internal negative dialogue at face value.

Even though your conscious mind will readily admit that not all of your automatic thoughts can possibly be true, expect your habitual unconscious to fight that notion strenuously. Thus, until your unconscious is thoroughly convinced, repeatedly tell yourself this irrefutable fact:

> *"Just because I think or feel something automatically, doesn't make it automatically valid."*

Note that there is no need to assume that you are wrong about everything. Just stop assuming that your automatic negative thoughts are always right. If you can do this, you will have figuratively tipped over the first of a series of dominoes. Your remaining victories will be won much more readily.

STEP 2:
IDENTIFY YOUR DISTORTED PERCEPTIONS AND DYSFUNCTIONAL RULES

Before you can replace your negative thinking habits with more constructive ones, you need to get good at recognizing your negative thoughts in the first place. This task becomes easier once you realize that there are only a limited number of them. General themes such as failure, rejection, financial security, and self-fulfillment are likely to occur many times.

Furthermore, regardless of their specific content, there are only two universal categories of negative statements that people make to themselves. The first category involves negative perceptions or observations about *specific* individuals or events in the present, past or future. The second category of negative thoughts includes universal rules and assumptions about people and life in *general*. To make the distinctions between the different types of negative thoughts more clear, consider the following list of examples:

Specific Perceptions

Future

"If I don't get this right, we are not going to prevail."

"How will I ever get this work done on time?"

"What if I embarrass myself?"

Present

"I don't spend any time with my family."

"The senior partners don't think I bill enough hours."

"I am not competent to take on this project."

Past

"What happened here was totally unfair."

"They never treated me with respect in that firm."

"She was always negative and insulting."

General Rules And Assumptions

"People are not trustworthy. They are all selfish."

"The only way to get it done is to do it yourself."

"Mistakes can't be tolerated because they lead to failure."

"There is nothing worse than being humiliated in public."

"Life is a jungle. Only the strong survive."

"Unpleasant situations need to be avoided at all costs."

"If you ignore problems they usually go away."

"Do things your way. Don't be controlled by others."

"You have to look out for yourself. No one else will."

Note that thoughts do not occur just in linguistic forms. They are experienced as visual, auditory and other types of sensory images as well. For example, instead of saying "I really blew this case", you may see yourself in a courtroom looking embarrassed. When you experience such images, translate them into linguistic thoughts.

There are times when your specific observations are objectively inaccurate. Let's call these *distorted perceptions*.

Similarly, there are times when your generalized assumptions don't lead you to desired results. Let's call these *dysfunctional rules*. Given the enormous effect that distorted perceptions and dysfunctional rules can have on your emotions and behaviors, it behooves you to identify and revise them whenever you can.

In the case of distorted negative perceptions, ask yourself to produce the evidence for them. Oftentimes, you will find that your specific observations about people and events in the past, the present, or the future are simply not grounded in fact. Sometimes such distortions are not based on any evidence at all. More than likely, however, perceptual distortions occur because facts are selectively filtered, exaggerated and overgeneralized. Such errors are often reflected in negative statements that include words like "always, never, terrible, awful, can't stand, absolutely must."

To illustrate how you might uncover a distorted perception, imagine that one day you find yourself repeating the following prediction: "I am going to totally blow this case." The anxious emotions and behaviors that such a thought is likely to create requires you to at least check its validity. Cross-examine yourself the same way that you would a witness. Say to yourself: "How do you know that you are going to blow this case even before it has begun? How many times has that happened to you in the past, even though you have said the same thing? Maybe, what you really mean is that you need more time to prepare. Your original statement is not based on fact; it is your own insecurity jumping to negative conclusions. You are paying an emotional price for it, so get yourself together and revise your original statement. The truth is that you just need more time to prepare."

Generalized beliefs, rules and assumptions are much more difficult to prove or disprove than perceptions. Often they are a matter of personal interpretation. In addition, frequently there are specific instances to which one can point that both support and refute a rule. For example, take a common rule like: "If you want something done right, do it yourself." All of us can point to instances in which someone to whom we delegated a task failed us. However, we also can point to instances in which we were more than satisfied with the work of another person.

To determine how often a rule is true, we would have to do an empirical study of some sort. However, proving or disproving the accuracy of a rule is not the practical thing to do. What is more relevant is to ask yourself whether your negative rules help you achieve positive results. Those that do not are dysfunctional.

For example, let us examine the functionality of believing that "if you want things done right, you do them yourself." One of the most important ramifications of living by this rule is that it encourages you not to delegate work. In turn, this means that you will not be an effective manager of other people. Ask yourself what kinds of lawyers tend to be more productive - effective delegators or those who do everything themselves? Similarly, consider what types of lawyers achieve senior partnerships or are successful at this role. Soon you might decide that even though your original belief contains a kernel of truth, it limits your ability to succeed as a lawyer and should be revised.

STEP 3:
CONSIDER ALTERNATIVE THOUGHTS

One of our most powerful cognitive abilities is to think dialectically. As you probably know, dialectics is a method of argument in which one purposefully weighs contradictory ideas. This ability is responsible for a great deal of human creativity and is much relied upon in the practice of law. It also happens to be the best way to break through a number of personal problems. Whenever you feel as though you are stuck in the mud emotionally, apply those same dialectical skills you use in thinking about legal matters to nonlegal ones.

The easiest way to generate alternative points of view is to simply consider the opposite of whatever your perceptions and rules might be. Another easy way is to take on the role of other people you know. Literally ask yourself, "What would .... say about this or how would he/she view it?" A variant of this is for you to take on the role of a different you. For example, if you tend to be a perfectionist, imagine yourself as someone who is competent but not bothered by mistakes. Then ask yourself the same question, "If I were this other person, how would I view this same situation?" You will be pleasantly surprised by how powerfully role playing loosens up your creativity.

STEP 4:
ASK AND ANSWER SOLUTION/FUTURE
ORIENTED QUESTIONS

Once you recognize your negative thoughts, evaluate their validity, appropriately revise the ones that are invalid and solve the problems suggested by the ones that are valid. For example, let us assume that you have been disturbed by the thought that your secretary does not like working for you. The best way to proceed is to first check out the validity of your thought and then do one of two things: If you are mistaken, simply change your opinion. If your are accurate, either get another secretary or look for ways to improve your relationship. The idea is to learn from the past and move on to a better future.

Many of the people who suffer from anxiety and depression do so in part because they fail to take this last step. When asked to confront their problems, they often report that they are doing so: "I think about my problems all of the time." They miss the point in that what they are actually doing is brooding over their problems. This only increases distress. Their thoughts deal with the past instead of the future. They focus on problems instead of solutions.

Once you have uncovered and validated a problem, the best way to move on is to ask yourself a series of solution/future oriented questions like:

How can I fix this?
What can I do about this now?
What can we do to improve matters?
How can we solve this problem in the future?

Many of us have a tendency to ask these questions in a rhetorical way. That is, the question mark is not real. We shrug our shoulders and say, "What can I do?" What we really intend to say is, "I can't do anything about this." Sentences that contain the word "can't" are often themselves automatic negative thoughts. Thus, if you catch yourself asking rhetorical questions, first try to simply place a real question mark at the end of your sentence and explore the answers you generate. If no answers are forthcoming, then treat your rhetorical question as a negative thought and go back to Step 1.

For example, here are some typical negative rhetorical questions that I have heard lawyers ask:

Where will our next client come from?
How do I ensure that the quality of our work is high?
How do we insure the future of this firm, given the competitive and changing nature of law practice?
How do I deal with partners who give me complex tasks, but no instruction, no training, no guidance, and no sympathy?

How do I deal with too many masters, when each of them
doesn't know or care what I am
doing for the others?
How can I make partner, when I don't really know what the
criteria or rules are?
What if I don't make partner?

These are all legitimate questions. My point is that they are
often asked in a rhetorical form. If you want to get rid of the
stress they cause, convert them into real questions and begin to
answer them in future/solution oriented ways.

For example, let us take the last question on the list, "What
if I don't make partner?" When you try to truly confront this
question, you may find that the reason you have been avoiding
the answer is that it often evokes other negative rhetorical
questions such as: "Will that mean that I am incompetent? In
turn, will that mean that I will not be able to get another good
job?" Once you uncover such thoughts, you will realize that
they are causing you much distress in the form of guilt and fear.
Don't avoid them. Place real question marks at the end of these
types of rhetorical questions and answer them.

MORE THAN JUST
HAPPY TALK

When you share your apprehensions with a well meaning friend or family member, the advice that you are most likely to get is: "Think positive. Everything will turn out for the better. You'll see." Essentially, this is a form of cheerleading in which the underlying message is: "Don't worry! Be happy!"

Sometimes this is the right advice. Many of us waste too much emotional energy anticipating negative events that never occur. If we would just "lighten up," life would be less stressful. Much of the time, however, this type of advice is both inappropriate and ineffective. In case you are confusing it with the advice I am giving you, allow me to distinguish the two.

"Happy talk" encourages you to ignore problems in the hope that they will disappear on their own. I am advising you to confront problems and fix them. "Happy talk" assumes that all negative emotions are dysfunctional and should be dismissed. I am advising you to assume that the evolutionary value of negative emotions is to draw your attention to your negative thoughts so that you can examine them more closely.

Undoubtedly, sometimes you will find that your negative thoughts have no foundation and should be revised. My advice calls on you to come to this conclusion only after you have fully examined them. However, there is the possibility that sometimes your negative thoughts will be valid and you will have good reason to feel angry, guilty or fearful. In such cases it then becomes your responsibility to make the necessary positive changes either in the environment or within yourself.

CONQUER YOUR
RESISTANCE TO CHANGE

Be prepared for several inner voices that will urge you to resist change. One of them will say: "This is too frustrating. I can't change." Indeed, at first your current thinking style may seem immutable and permanent. Again, this will occur because your old thought patterns are exceedingly well-learned habits that have taken many years to develop. They have become as automatic as walking up a staircase. In fact, the core of the problem is that they are too automatic and need to be switched into manual. Don't expect a transition to occur without effort.

No matter how unchangeable your habitual thoughts may appear, remember that they are learned patterns of behavior. To my knowledge, few theorists argue that humans are born with specific ideas in their brains such as, "What if I lose this case?" Such thoughts are learned, not inborn. No matter how well-learned they are, they can be unlearned. It is just a matter of time, practice, and the right techniques. Furthermore, once you get going old habits become increasingly easier to break.

Another likely inner voice tempting you to quit will say, "I don't have time to do this now. I'll face up to my problems tomorrow." Of course, the next day you wind up saying the same thing. Whenever you catch yourself thinking this way, switch your focus to the lifelong pain you will feel if you fail to do anything about your overly stressful existence. Literally make a list in your mind: constant time pressures, low job satisfaction, anger, fear, misgivings about your personal life, heart disease, etc. Contrast that against what you will gain if you "bite the bullet" now: less psychological pressure, better physical health, higher self-esteem, greater job satisfaction, positive relationships with associates, spouse and children, etc. This will help you conclude that change is not only possible, but also well worth the price.

Finally, the most insidious of your inner voices may call out and say to you, "If I admit that my thinking style in the past has been erroneous, then I will have to live with the idea that I have failed in some way. Also, what if I try to change and don't succeed?" Notice that these types of negative predictions and conclusions will evoke fear of failure in you, which in turn will tempt you to quit. No thoughts are more harmful than those that prevent you from growing. Let them be your first targets. Argue against such ideas as you would in a legal brief or a case. Here are two sample responses: "First, it is more functional to think of the past as learning experiences, not failures. Second, if you don't change, then you will wind up failing in the future as well as in the past. Is that what you want?"

What if you try and don't succeed? You try again! And after that, you keep trying as many times as it takes to succeed. The only reason not to try is if you honestly think that you are so defective in some way as to be incapable of change. If you think that, however, then you owe it to yourself to evaluate the validity of such a conclusion by seeing a mental health professional.

SECTION V

HEED

YOUR

EMOTIONS

By starving emotions we become humorless, rigid and stereotyped; by repressing them we become literal, reformatory and holier-than-thou; encouraged they perfume life; discouraged they poison it.

Joseph Collins

The quality of strength lined with tenderness is an unbeatable combination.

Maya Angelou

HEED YOUR EMOTIONS?

"Hear reason, or she'll make you feel her."
Benjamin Franklin

My task in this chapter is formidable. I am going to advise you to become more aware of your emotions, knowing that lawyers tend to have a low regard for "emotional" people. Current national statistics show that the vast majority of lawyers characterize themselves as thinkers who prefer to make decisions and solve problems on the basis of logical analysis rather than feelings.[56] Indeed, this rationalist view, which has its roots in Greek and British philosophers, is greatly valued and ingrained in American law. Yet, I want to dissuade you from it.

Although my purpose is to help you take control of your negative emotions, I know that the words "emotional" and "control" may seem incompatible to you. Like many lawyers, your idea of controlling negative emotions may be to deny or suppress them. Thus, your initial desire may be for someone to teach you how to subdue your emotions even more than you do now, not accentuate them. Permit me to explain why this is a mistake.

We humans are genetically wired with the ability to use our negative emotions as informational signals of our own distress. In other words, emotions are like finely calibrated indicator gauges. The only difference is that you don't see these gauges, you feel them. They capture your attention by creating pain and suffering, and that helps you determine just how serious the situation is. The more emotional pain you feel, the more seriously you consider your distress. From an evolutionary standpoint, this design has survival value; by feeling our distress, we become more likely to pay attention to it, reflect on it, and do something about it.

Denying or suppressing your emotions makes about as much sense as choosing to ignore a fire alarm. Unless you listen to the alarm and acknowledge the fact that there is a fire, you are very likely to get burned. Furthermore, the appropriate response to a fire alarm is not to turn it off, but to put out the fire that turned it on. Similarly, to reduce your stress you need to become more aware of your internal signals of distress in the first place. Then, you can reduce your distress by altering the thoughts or the environmental events that cause your negative emotions.

The many challenges lawyers face arouse powerful emotions that cause a great deal of stress and can lead to both mental and physical illnesses. Permanent improvements require emotional self-awareness. This is difficult enough for anyone to do, but it is especially difficult if you are of the opinion that it is the wrong thing to do. Actually, it is the right thing to do.

INTELLIGENT PEOPLE ARE
EMOTIONALLY AWARE

If you are like the majority of lawyers, you probably believe that whereas reason and logic are higher order abilities, emotions are vestiges of our biological ties to lower forms of life. This point of view assumes that people who rely on their intellect rather than on their emotions, are more likely to be successful. The idea sounds incontrovertible at first, but it begins to falter when the following question is raised: Why is it that so many brilliant people we know do so poorly?

In a highly acclaimed and well researched book, Daniel Goleman[57] makes the point that emotional awareness is just as much a predictor of success as intellectual ability. Our common definition of intelligence, he argues, is too narrow. In reality, abilities such as self-awareness, empathy, determination, social skills, motivation, and impulse control are facets of what he calls "emotional intelligence." People who excel both intellectually and emotionally, and who integrate these two realms, are the truly gifted among us.

EMOTIONS REVEAL YOUR LOGIC

The traditional view is that emotions and thoughts are separate entities, and that emotions have a disorganizing and interfering influence on rational thought and behavior. This is a myth, however. It underestimates the adaptive powers of millions of years of evolution and misrepresents how we humans actually function.[58] Actually, thoughts and emotions are elements of the same experiential continuum. As discussed in previous chapters, the stream of human experience is composed of the following sequence of elements:

Stimulus > Thought > Emotion > Behavior

Viewing thoughts and emotions as if they are distinct entities is like breaking down a golf swing into parts. The idea that you can experience a thought free of emotion or an emotion devoid of thought is a myth. Emotions always reflect our thoughts and energize our bodily behaviors. For example, only when we *think* we have been wronged do we *feel* angry, and only when we *feel* angry do we *behave* in a hostile manner.

It is not accurate to characterize emotions as bad or primitive, or to assume that they have a disruptive effect on logic. Most of the time, emotions do not have a disruptive effect on our reasoning. On the contrary, they usually help us focus our mental attention and energize our goal oriented behaviors.

At times all of us experience dysfunctional emotions that defy reason and lead to regretful behaviors. However, it is not correct to assume that the emotions are to blame. Illogical thoughts are what cause dysfunctional emotions in the first place. Emotions are extensions of thoughts and are only as logical and reasonable as the thoughts that precede them.

Becoming more aware of your emotions does not make you less logical and more soft headed. On the contrary, to be truly aware of your emotions you must understand the thoughts that cause them. Once you understand your own thoughts, you can evaluate their logic. This makes you smarter.

EMOTIONS REVEAL YOUR GOALS

To be successful in any area of life, you first need to know what you want. The question this raises for most people is, "How do I figure out what I want?" Obviously, one way is to make a list of the options you have and their pros and cons, and then to choose between them. So far, the process sounds like it is based on reasoned logic. By what measure, however, do you determine the weights that you give each of the pros and cons? In the final analysis, most of us do this through our emotions. That is, we make our final choices on the basis of how we think certain outcomes are going to make us feel.

For example, consider why you would ever want to become a partner in a law firm. Typically, lawyers give a number of reasons for wanting partnership, but let us focus just on the financial rewards that it brings. You might think this is a silly question, but ask yourself, "Why do I want higher financial rewards?" Obviously, it allows you to buy bigger and better material things and send your children to more prestigious colleges. But then, ask yourself, "Why do I want these things to begin with?" By continuing to ask such questions, you will ultimately come to the point where you realize that the bottom line is in how it makes you feel. That is, the driving forces behind the motive to achieve financial success are such feelings as self-esteem, joy, security, and power.

Through evolution, most of us are naturally wired to do that which results in the pleasure of positive emotions and that which avoids the pain of negative emotions. This hedonistic model of human nature holds that the design of our physiological and psychological systems are very similar. In the same way that the physical pain caused by touching a flame drives us to avoid fire, pain that is caused by guilt and shame motivates us to refrain from violating our values.

Because of their ability to create pain and pleasure, emotions are the driving forces behind our most basic goals in life. What distinguishes us from each other, is that we differ in what triggers our various emotions. For some, giving a final argument in front of a jury is exhilarating, whereas for others it is frightening.

There are times when certain choices create mixed feelings. For example, part of you may want the positive feelings that partnership brings, but another voice in you realizes the sacrifices involved and feels guilty and fearful about what it will do to your family. This type of conflict is very painful, but it does motivate you to reach resolution. Ignoring your internal conflicts tends to result in a mixed bag of behaviors that do not accomplish either set of desires in optimal fashion.

In summary, if you want to know what makes you and others tick, pay attention to emotions. The ultimate reason we do or don't do certain things in life is because of the way we think it will make us feel emotionally. All of us share one ultimate goal: to avoid negative emotions and evoke positive ones. Thus, for example, if you are not doing something you "should," you can be fairly certain that it is because you are associating that action with some type of negative emotion, such as fear. Change can only occur when you accurately diagnose the problem and then do that which is necessary to alter the emotion.

HOW TO RECOGNIZE YOUR DISTRESSFUL EMOTIONS

Many lawyers have a tendency to answer questions about emotions with words that relate to thoughts. For example, if asked, "How did this event make you *feel*?", many lawyers reply with, "I *thought* it was unfair," instead of, "It made me *feel* angry." Lawyers who have learned to suppress their emotions this way often need to relearn what they feel like and what they are called.

Like hues on a color wheel, the number of emotions we are capable of feeling is extensive. While it is not my aim to discuss them all, I want to focus your attention on three primary negative emotions that are often implicated in the kind of stress that lawyers experience: fear, anger and guilt. These are not only among the most common of the stress producing emotions, but they are also among the most harmful to your health. I urge you to become proficient at recognizing them in yourself.

FEAR OF FAILURE & REJECTION

Given the adversarial nature of our legal system and how costly mistakes can be, fear is a frequent emotion among lawyers. Two kinds of fear are particularly common: fear of failure and fear of rejection. Fear of failure might be evoked by thoughts like: "If this argument doesn't fly, then we will lose this case." Fear of rejection is likely to be triggered by thoughts such as: "The loss of this client will not go over well at the next partner's meeting." Because failure often leads to rejection, both kinds of fears frequently get evoked simultaneously.

Each of us experiences fear from time to time and it has adaptive value. Without fear, we would be more likely to do things that are dangerous. Fear is dysfunctional, however, when it is unjustifiably strong or chronic. In addition to causing unnecessary distress, fear can be very harmful in other ways. It can cause you to anticipate harm where there is none and thus distort your perceptions and judgments. Often, fear results in your avoiding situations that you need to confront. In addition, it can cause you to feel guilty about your "cowardice" and lead to low self-esteem and depression.

For example, I have known several lawyers who feared losing or being humiliated so much that they developed a strong aversion to litigation. Instead of confronting and overcoming their fears, they made it a habit to avoid litigation as much as possible. They developed elaborate justifications to make it appear as though important decisions about cases were based solely on facts. Secretly, however, many of their decisions were based on unjustifiable fears. Not only did they fear litigation, but they also dreaded the thought that someone would discover their lack of courage. Distress and low self-esteem were their constant companions. You can imagine how it affected their careers and personal lives.

ANGER AND HOSTILITY

Having listened to my opinion that he was too distrusting of people and socially isolated, a lawyer-client of mine once jokingly said to me: "Doc, just because I'm paranoid doesn't mean that people aren't out to get me." He was referring to the fact that our legal system encourages antagonism and brings out the worst in people. Indeed, as a national group, lawyers are more suspicious, cynical, authoritarian, dogmatic, aggressive and Machiavellian than the general population.[59] These are all components of anger and hostility.

Obviously, my client was right that our legal system is by design intended to encourage adversarial behavior. It is also logical to assume that many of the people who are attracted to the practice of law must not be averse to human conflict. Some may actually seek it. In combination, these two factors make anger a very commonly felt emotion among lawyers.

Perhaps, the anger that you experience is a significant part of what you mean when you report that your job is stressful. On the other hand, you may not be fully aware of the hostility you harbor within. For example, I know that some of my lawyer-clients see themselves as realistic, not cynical. Furthermore, they are not always cognizant of how often they feel and act irritated and impatient. In some cases only something like a spouse's threat of divorce shocks them into awareness.

In addition to being highly unpleasant, anger appears to be harmful to your physical health.[60] Take, for example, a study done in 1985, in which a group of researchers contacted 118 lawyers who had been law students at the University of North Carolina in 1956 and 1957, and who had completed a personality test for another unrelated research project.[61] It turned out that their scores on a hostility scale many years earlier were very predictive of their mortality rates. Less than 5 percent of those with the lowest hostility scores had died by 1985. In contrast, lawyers with the highest hostility scores had a 20 percent death rate.

GUILT IS ANGER
DIRECTED AT YOURSELF

Anger and guilt can be thought of as very similar emotions. We feel anger when we criticize others and guilt when we condemn ourselves. That is, when we point to another person and say, "You! It's your fault!," it is usually an expression of anger. When we point to ourselves and say, "Me! It's my fault!," it often is an expression of guilt.

The relationship between anger and guilt was pointed out to me by one of my clients many years ago. After listening to her complain about her spouse for several sessions, I gently suggested that the chronic level of anger she felt towards him was both unhealthy and ineffective. She swiftly replied that by holding on to her anger she was able to prevent the pain of depression. When asked what would cause her to be depressed, she listed a number of regrets about herself. "You mean that you would feel guilty about who you are?," I said. "Yes," she said partly in jest, "if I didn't blame him for my problems, who else could I blame?"

Many of us associate guilt with moral transgressions that arouse one's conscience, but it is also an emotion that gets triggered when your image of an ideal self does not match with your perception of a true self. Guilt does get evoked when you violate ethical values. But, it also occurs when you think that you do not measure up to other types of values. For example, people who do not think that they are as successful as they "should" be, tend to feel guilty.

Chronic feelings of guilt can lead to low self-esteem and eventually to depression. In turn, this can lead to lower productivity, sleep disorders and various physical ailments that are brought on by a less active immune system.[62]

Many lawyers feel guilt much more often than they express it. One source is the general public's disrespectful image of lawyers as a group who will do anything to win a case, regardless of its morality and sometimes legality, purely for material gain and status. What makes it worse is that many attorneys have similar thoughts themselves about their own and their profession's practices.[63]

Another source of guilt for lawyers is that many tend to be perfectionistic thinkers. Since perfection cannot be achieved, striving for perfection causes chronic dissatisfaction with oneself. Perfectionistic lawyers also have difficulty knowing when to let go of their work and tend to become workaholics. I will never forget what a lawyer-client disclosed to me once in this regard. After several sessions of prodding and digging, I said to him, "You sound like you feel guilty about something other than what we have been discussing." He became very pensive and then revealed to me and to himself for the first time: "I think I feel guilty about not having had a heart attack yet. In our office, it is like a badge of honor. It means that you are a hard worker. Sounds crazy, doesn't it?"

Perfectionism and workaholism also interfere with family life. A great many lawyers feel guilty about not paying enough attention to family matters. Both genders feel this way, but female attorneys are particularly likely to do so because they experience greater role conflicts.

ADVICE

FOR

MENTALLY

IMPAIRED

LAWYERS

Although the world is full of suffering, it's also full of the overcoming of it.

Helen Keller

It is with disease of the mind, as with those of the body; we are half dead before we understand our disorder, and half cured when we do.

Charles Caleb Colton

CONFRONT YOUR MENTAL IMPAIRMENTS

"The mass of [people] lead lives of quiet desperation."
Henry David Thoreau

As detailed elsewhere in this book, the data on mentally impaired lawyers are very alarming. They indicate that lawyers are at a significantly higher risk for developing depression or problem drinking than the general population. Obviously, these ailments damage lawyers and their families. In addition, they diminish lawyers' ability to serve clients and often lead to violations of professional practice standards and malpractice.

Unfortunately, the stigmas associated with mental illnesses or substance abuse disorders makes these ailments difficult to confront. Fearing that they will be thought of as lacking personal control or character, many lawyers deny that they have a problem and live with it as long as possible. Unfortunately, denial doesn't make things go away. It often makes things get much worse and exacts a heavy price - emotionally, professionally and financially. This section is designed to help mentally impaired attorneys confront their problems.

The next several chapters outline the legal issues mentally impaired attorneys need to face, describe what can be done about depression and alcohol abuse, and recommend how and where to get help and more information. Depression and alcohol abuse are singled out for discussion because they are the most common stress-related ailments. Although much more in-depth information on these and other mental health problems is available elsewhere and should be consulted, this section is a good starting point for impaired attorneys themselves, as well as their colleagues, friends and family members.

LEGAL QUESTIONS FACING MENTALLY IMPAIRED LAWYERS

by Douglas B. Marlowe, Ph.D., J.D.

Lawyers with psychological problems are often hesitant to get help because they worry about such issues as confidentiality, liability and job security. To some extent, the types of concerns they have depend on whether their treatment is purely voluntary, or whether it is being mandated by disciplinary authorities. Not surprisingly, greater protections exist for individuals who are in the former category. For this reason it is always advisable to seek help proactively, before an impairment has had a significant effect on one's professional functioning.

This chapter addresses the most common legal questions facing lawyers in either elective or mandated treatment. A final section deals with what colleagues and employers of impaired attorneys are obligated to do. This is only an introductory outline of the issues. Lawyers with serious concerns regarding any issues covered here will require a more thorough review of the law in their jurisdictions. Local Lawyer Assistance Programs (LAPs) or the American Bar Association's Commission on Lawyer Assistance Programs are good resources for this type of information. For more details on contacting these resources, see the last chapter in this section.

THE ELECTIVE TREATMENT CONTEXT

Is Treatment Confidential?

Note that whereas laws covering the confidentiality of substance abuse and mental health treatment do have much in common, in many jurisdictions they are not identical.

Protections for mental health treatment information are largely governed by state law. The confidentiality of substance abuse treatment information, however, is most often controlled by federal laws[64] enacted in the 1970's, requiring a higher level of protection of such information.

Information disclosed during substance abuse or mental health counseling receives strict privilege and confidentiality protections. These protections are derived from professional ethical standards[65] as well as from testimonial privileges that attach in many states to communications with licensed psychologists, psychiatrists, social workers, or other professionals.[66] The United States Supreme Court recently held that a psychotherapist-patient privilege exists under federal common-law, which applies at least to communications with licensed clinicians.[67]

Federal and state laws also provide broad content-based protections for substance abuse and mental health records held in regulated treatment facilities. These protections are triggered by the nature of the information, and are not dependent on the professional identity of the service provider. Without the written informed consent of the client, substance abuse and mental health treatment information may be disclosed only to treatment providers in an emergency, third party payers or financial auditors, judicial officials in the course of civil commitment and similar types of legal proceedings, or pursuant to a court order.[68] There are also provisions for nonconsensual disclosure of such information to proper authorities when patients are a danger to themselves or others, or when it is necessary to report child abuse or neglect.

Bar or court sanctioned Lawyer Assistance Programs (LAP) are now available in every jurisdiction to help provide impaired lawyers with peer support and professional intervention.[69] Generally, communications between an impaired lawyer and LAP staff or volunteers are strictly confidential, either by virtue of laws that protect all substance abuse or mental health treatment information, or through separate statutes or court rules that apply specifically to LAPs in a given jurisdiction.[70]

Informed consent forms for the release of substance abuse or mental health information should clearly specify who is permitted to release and to receive the information, the purpose of the disclosure, and how much and what kind of information may be disclosed.[71] They should indicate that consent is revocable at-will, and specify a date, event, or condition upon which consent automatically expires.

Each disclosure of substance abuse information should be accompanied by a specific "prohibition on redisclosure" provision which puts the recipient on notice that he or she, too, is bound by legal confidentiality standards.[72] Consensual disclosure to one party does not imply that disclosure is permitted to other parties, nor does it reduce the confidential nature of the information. Some states have similar provisions for the release of some types of mental health information.[73]

When governed by Federal laws, substance abuse treatment information cannot be used to initiate a criminal investigation or to substantiate criminal charges against a patient. Most states do not explicitly provide parallel criminal justice protections for mental health treatment information.

Must I Acknowledge My Impairment On A Bar Application?

ABA Model Rule 8.1 requires Bar applicants to respond truthfully and completely on admissions materials. This can be problematic for questions relating to mental illness and substance abuse. In 1994, the ABA House of Delegates resolved that Bar questions should be narrowly tailored to focus on current fitness to practice law, and should not unduly discourage applicants from seeking assistance. Several courts[74] have found that this principle is inherent in the protections accorded mentally impaired individuals under the *Americans with Disabilities Act*.[75] From these cases, it appears that it may be unnecessary to prove actual discrimination in response to an endorsement of such Bar items. The mere existence of the questions may be interpreted in certain instances as imposing additional regulatory burdens upon the disabled.[76]

Fitness determinations may, however, inquire about conduct or related impairments that might affect an applicant's current ability to practice. If a pattern of unstable or questionable behavior emerges, the Admissions Board is entitled to inquire further about possible substance abuse or mental illness, and to make necessary referrals for further assessment or treatment.[77]

Given My Impairment, Can I Be Admitted To The Bar, Get A Job And Be Supported In Overcoming My Limitations?

The *Americans with Disabilities Act* (ADA)[78] provides broad anti-discrimination protections for individuals with disabilities. The term "disability" encompasses any physical or mental impairment that substantially limits one or more major life activity. It extends protections contained in Section 504 of the *Rehabilitation Act of 1973*[79] to public employers, private employers of 15 or more people, and professional regulatory boards. The Board of Bar Examiners is a public entity within the meaning of the ADA,[80] and in most states protections therefore apply to Bar admissions determinations.

Disabled persons are entitled to "reasonable accommodations" that assist them in meeting employment demands. Employers are excused from making accommodations that impose an "undue hardship," requiring excessive effort and expense in light of the financial and other resources of the employer. Accommodation is also not required if the employee poses a significant risk to the health and safety of other individuals. Although employers do not have an obligation to eliminate stresses that are inherent in the job, accommodations may include part time or modified work schedules to reduce job-related stress or facilitate attendance in treatment.[81] Note that accommodation is not required if it is not requested.

Current users of illegal drugs are exempted from ADA protections.[82] Discrimination is prohibited, however, if the individual has completed or is enrolled in a drug abuse rehabilitation program and there is significant evidence to show that he or she has achieved abstinence. To verify abstinence, employers may institute drug-testing programs for identified substance abusers. There is no protection for relapse during the course of rehabilitation, even if the relapse is of short duration and does not affect job performance. Protections are unavailable if a lapse occurred recently enough to justify a reasonable belief that drug use may be intermittent or on-going.[83]

The Equal Employment Opportunity Commission (EEOC) has opined that the stresses associated with family and employment problems are not covered by the ADA unless they are of sufficient severity to meet diagnostic criteria for a recognized mental disorder.[84] Thus, to avail oneself of the protections accorded by the ADA, proper diagnosis and treatment by a mental health professional is often required.

RIGHTS AND RESPONSIBILITIES IN
THE DISCIPLINARY CONTEXT

If impairment has already contributed to professional misconduct or unfitness, the status of being mentally ill or substance dependent does not shield the attorney from the consequences of his or her actions. It may, however, trigger a set of procedural safeguards and dispositional options that permit the attorney to receive appropriate treatment and to resume the safe and effective practice of law.

Are Impairments Disclosed At Disciplinary Proceedings Confidential?

In a growing number of states, complaints submitted to a lawyer disciplinary board can become a matter of public record at a fairly early stage of the process, soon after the initial investigations are completed. Once it has been determined that there was a violation of a professional standard, the state's highest court may order a public censure or public reprimand of an attorney, or may post a public notice that the attorney has been placed on inactive status. In particular, disciplinary matters that are predicated upon an attorney's conviction of a crime are generally not confidential. Similarly, if an attorney is declared to be incapacitated from practicing law due to mental illness, infirmity, or addiction to drugs or alcohol, the state disciplinary board is normally required to post a public notice of the attorney's transfer to inactive status. A notice of public discipline or transfer to inactive status is also transmitted to the ABA National Discipline Data Bank.

If My Infractions Are Caused By Mental Impairments, Will I Retain My License?

Most jurisdictions offer some variant of probation for attorneys who are convicted of relatively minor infractions of professional rules of conduct.[85] This requires a showing that the continued practice of law by the respondent would be unlikely to harm the public or to cause the courts or legal profession to fall into disrepute. In most jurisdictions, evidence of substance abuse or mental illness is viewed as material to this finding, and counseling for such problems is an ordinary condition of probation.[86] Largely as a result of social or historical forces, however, probationary schemes in many states are quite explicit and detailed with regard to substance abuse, but are more general or vague with regard to other mental impairments.

Respondents are generally required to demonstrate a causal link between professional misconduct and mental impairment. With regard to substance abuse, many states require a demonstration that "but for" such impairment, the misconduct would not have occurred.[87] Substance abuse does not have to be the sole cause of the misconduct, but it must have been a substantial factor. Other states only require a showing that substance abuse was "a factor" in causing the misconduct.[88] For both chemical dependency and mental disability, the ABA recommends license reinstatement if the impairment "caused" the misconduct, there is evidence of "sustained" recovery, and recovery has "arrested" the misconduct.[89]

Is Treatment And Related Types Of Information Shared With Disciplinary Authorities?

A common condition of probation requires the impaired attorney to execute any written authorization that is necessary for the Disciplinary Board to verify compliance with treatment.

Substance abuse probationers are typically required to abstain from all classes of mood-altering or mind-altering chemicals, to regularly attend Alcoholics Anonymous (AA) or another designated treatment program, to undergo any treatment procedure prescribed or recommended by a physician or addiction counselor, and to authorize verification of attendance and compliance with treatment. These restrictive conditions may not explicitly attach by statute to cases involving mental illness. However, mandatory psychological counseling and periodic progress reports to the Disciplinary Board are appropriate conditions of probation in most cases. The permissible scope of disclosure is generally limited to a brief description of the treatment program as well as a brief statement regarding the client's attendance, prognosis, and progress in therapy.

A "practice monitor" or "financial monitor" may be appointed to temporarily oversee an attorney's practice, to secure client funds, or to control financial decisions. In most states, a "sobriety monitor" may also be appointed for attorneys placed on substance abuse probation. In Pennsylvania, for instance, the sobriety monitor meets in person with each respondent at least twice per month and maintains weekly telephone contact throughout the probationary period. He or she files quarterly progress reports with the Disciplinary Board and is required to immediately report any probation violations.

When an attorney's impairment leads to criminal liability, the release of treatment information may also be a condition of criminal probation. For example, an addicted lawyer might be charged with possession of a controlled substance. Federal regulations permit substance abuse information to be disclosed to criminal justice authorities who have made participation in a treatment program a condition of probation, parole, or a similar disposition.[90] Disclosure must be limited to those individuals having a specific need for the information in connection with their duty to monitor the client's progress, and must be limited in scope to that which is necessary to permit adequate monitoring. As noted earlier, this information may not be used to substantiate or initiate criminal charges against the client. It may only be used to verify compliance with probationary conditions. Unfortunately, state laws are often silent with regard to disclosure of mental health information in criminal justice contexts.

DEALING WITH IMPAIRED COLLEAGUES

ABA Model Rule 8.3 requires attorneys to report professional misconduct or unfitness on the part of colleagues. This Rule was amended, however, in 1991 to protect the confidentiality of information disclosed to a fellow attorney within an approved lawyers assistance program (LAP).[91] Rule 8.3(c) treats such information as if it were subject to the attorney-client privilege.

Professional ethical standards may also require a lawyer to take affirmative measures to deal with an unfit colleague. ABA Model Rule 5.1 requires partners and supervisory lawyers to institute reasonable remedial measures for impaired employees. The ABA strongly encourages law firms to develop employee assistance programs (EAP), and has approved of confidentiality protections in the identification, treatment, and rehabilitation of impaired law firm personnel.[92]

As was discussed earlier, The *Americans with Disabilities Act* (ADA)[93] requires all public employers and all private employers of 15 or more people to make "reasonable accommodations" that assist the mentally impaired in meeting employment demands. However, employers do not have to make accommodations that impose an "undue hardship" on their resources. In addition, accommodation is not required in cases where an impaired employee poses a significant risk to the health and safety of other individuals. Employers are not required to eliminate stresses that are an integral part of the job, but under some circumstances they may be required to offer part time or modified work schedules as a way of reducing job-related stress or facilitating attendance in treatment.[94] No accommodation is required unless it is requested.

ALCOHOLISM: SYMPTOMS, CAUSES & TREATMENTS

by Douglas B. Marlowe, Ph.D., J.D.

Alcoholism exacts an exorbitant toll on lawyers, the legal system, and consumers of legal services. In a 1990 study[95] conducted by the North Carolina Bar Association, a staggering 17% of the 2,600 attorneys surveyed admitted to drinking 3-5 alcoholic beverages per day. In the state of Washington, another study[96] found that 18% of the 801 lawyers surveyed were problem drinkers. It is estimated that the number of lawyers in the United States actively abusing alcohol and drugs is twice that of the general population.[97] Approximately 40% to 70% of attorney disciplinary proceedings and malpractice actions are linked to alcohol abuse or a mental illness.[98]

Yet, despite this high incidence, lawyers suffering from alcoholism often feel painfully alone. Fearing discovery or retribution, they are reticent to ask questions or to attempt to learn more about their problem. Very often, they fail to seek help before the problem has escalated to serious proportions. The purpose of this chapter is to introduce the impaired lawyer to the symptoms and causes of alcohol dependence and to the large menu of treatment options that now exist. This information also should be of help to colleagues, friends and family members of alcohol dependent attorneys.

THE SYMPTOMS

"Denial" is a common feature of alcoholism.[99] There are widely differing opinions about whether denial is an unconscious psychological defense mechanism, a misguided effort to conceal the shame of addiction, or simply a reaction to accusations or punitive actions by other people. Regardless, it is clear that those who are addicted to alcohol are often the last ones to recognize or acknowledge the existence of a problem. As a result, they unfortunately may not seek help until they are faced with serious medical, legal, financial, or social repercussions.

Official diagnostic criteria for "alcoholism" or "alcohol dependence" focus on the compulsive use of alcohol despite the significant negative consequences of that use.[100] Some alcoholics will exhibit symptoms of physical dependence, including a need for significantly increasing amounts of alcohol to achieve the desired effect ("tolerance"), or withdrawal symptoms (e.g., nausea, tremor, insomnia) when levels of alcohol in the blood decline.

For a substantial proportion of alcoholics, however, dependence is manifested solely by a behavioral or psychological compulsion to use alcohol, without any noticeable accompanying physical symptoms. This may include recurrent episodes of binge drinking; frequent intoxication under dangerous or inappropriate circumstances (e.g., while driving); multiple, unsuccessful efforts to quit or to reduce the use of alcohol; excessive involvement in alcohol-related activities; reduced involvement in adaptive or productive social and occupational activities; or the continued use of alcohol despite significant physical or psychological ill-effects.

Rather than focusing on these direct symptoms of addiction, however, it is often more instructive or productive to focus on the loss of functions or competencies that typically accompany the addiction.[101] Efforts to confront an alcoholic with positive evidence of his or her addiction (e.g., black-outs, binges, or the smell of liquor on the breath) typically invoke excuses, manipulations, or angry counter-attacks. It is much harder, however, to deny the existence of a problem when one's accomplishments have fallen far short of one's goals and abilities.

THEORIES OF CAUSATION

Theories about the causes and treatment of alcoholism are generally more reflective of personal philosophies and belief systems than of scientific or clinical evidence. Historically, the "Moral Model" of addiction viewed alcoholism as a sign of characterological weakness or moral turpitude. As such, treatment, if any, was designed to confront the alcoholic with the consequences of his or her behaviors and to force or shame him or her into making improvements.

The "Disease Model" of addiction assumed prominence in the middle part of this century. This model, which views alcoholism as fundamentally a medical illness, has found some support from recent discoveries about the genetic, biochemical, and pharmacological aspects of addiction. Treatments based upon the Disease Model sometimes emphasize the individual's relative powerlessness over the illness. This philosophy has attracted a great deal of support from the "self-help" movement because of its deemphasis on issues of blame and morality.

Most recently, a "Habit Model" or "Behavioral Model" of addiction has achieved relative prominence, particularly in the fields of psychology and education. This model views addiction as essentially a learned behavior, resulting from faulty problem solving, ineffective role modeling, or a complicated system of rewards and punishments which sustains the alcohol usage.[102] Rather than viewing the individual as powerless in the face of a disease process, the Behavioral Model seeks to increase the individual's sense of efficacy and potential control over the problem. A distinction is made between moral blameworthiness regarding the past and behavioral accountability in the future. People may not "choose" to be addicted, but it is assumed that they have ultimate control over changing their behavioral patterns.

Philosophies aside, no one really knows for certain what causes alcoholism and it is highly unlikely that any single causal agent will ever be identified. Alcoholism appears to be a result of many different processes. For any particular individual, it may stem from a genetic predisposition, from environmental stress or trauma, from learning history, or from a complex combination of any of these.

It is useful to think about alcoholism in light of the "diathesis-stress" model of illness.[103] Some individuals have a strong genetic loading ("diathesis") for a particular disease, which may be activated with minimal environmental influence. For example, some people are genetically predisposed to develop cancer, which may manifest itself almost irrespective of diet, exercise, or other habits. Other individuals, in contrast, are genetically heartier and do not develop the disease unless they are exposed to potent environmental carcinogens. In a similar vein, individuals appear to vary in their genetic vulnerability to alcoholism. Some people can apparently drink steadily without developing dependence or becoming socially maladapted. Others are less fortunate.

Given the current state of medical science, it is difficult to know in advance who is or is not vulnerable to developing alcoholism. However, a look at your family tree may shed light on your own risk liability. Rates of alcoholism are significantly higher within some families than in the general population.[104] It is uncertain whether this is due to an inherited familial vulnerability to alcoholism, or whether it results from role modeling or social learning. Children of alcoholics may simply be exposed to alcohol at a younger age, or they may be negatively affected by concomitant family dysfunction.[105] Most likely, a positive family history reflects both learned and genetic factors, in which biological and environmental forces combine to increase one's risk exponentially.

Compared to the general population, alcoholics suffer from significantly higher rates of psychiatric disorders such as depression and anxiety. This has led to some speculation that alcoholics might be "self-medicating" some uncomfortable emotional state.[106] In fact, part of the chemical effect of alcohol is to dull the emotions. It is difficult, however, to disentangle cause and effect because of alcohol's depressant influence on the central nervous system.[107] Chronic alcohol use may bring about long-term brain changes, leading to the development of depressive or anxiety states. It is also possible that some individuals have a generalized vulnerability to stress which, depending on the specific circumstances, may manifest itself as alcoholism, depression, anxiety, or some other emotional disturbance.

TREATMENT OPTIONS

Regardless of the counseling option one chooses, it is always highly advisable to first undergo a thorough physical evaluation by a physician. A number of complicating medical conditions often accompany chronic alcohol abuse which, paradoxically, may be exacerbated by withdrawal from or sudden reduction in alcohol use.[108] In addition, a physician can address other related difficulties such as vitamin deficiencies that may contribute to a more difficult recovery.

A dizzying array of specific treatment options are available for alcohol dependence. Many practitioners tout their particular program as being most effective for most clients under most circumstances. Unfortunately, these superlatives tend to confuse consumers and to cause needless dissension within the addictions field. The consumer of addiction services should attempt to find the best match for his or her needs and comfort level. Just like shopping for a suit, not all styles are an appropriate fit. If you are uncomfortable with or disillusioned by one treatment choice, do some additional research and consider other options. Several books are available which provide fairly balanced appraisals of different treatment options, including synopses of empirical evidence (if any) supporting the efficacy of these programs.[109]

Treatment programs differ along many dimensions, including: their causal and treatment philosophies (i.e., Moral Model, Disease Model, or Behavioral Model); whether they are conducted in an inpatient, outpatient or residential setting; whether they are administered by licensed professionals or by peers who are themselves in recovery; and whether they are performed in an individual, group, or family therapy format.

Traditionally, alcoholism was treated in an inpatient or residential setting. The first week or so was generally dedicated to "detoxifying" the individual or reducing withdrawal symptoms (if any), followed by a structured routine of group and recreational therapies. The emphasis was generally placed on preventing the individual's contact with alcohol or alcohol-related stimuli.

Although this may be an effective mode of intervention in the very short term, it also may not adequately prepare an individual for returning to life in the "real world," with all of its associated stressors and triggers for relapse. Being away from the familiarity of family, friends, and job may itself cause additional stress and feelings of loneliness. Social and occupational demands continue to pile up during this absence, and family tensions may be intensified. These and other considerations have led to a greater reliance on outpatient treatment for those individuals who do not have severe medical or psychiatric complications accompanying their alcohol use.[110]

Outpatient treatment enables the individual to practice strategies and skills learned in therapy in the "real world" and to bring new material and actual experiences into the therapy sessions.[111] For individuals with more severe addictions, this may be accomplished in a day or partial hospital program in which therapeutic services are provided for several hours during the day or evening, after which the individual returns home for the night.

In either an inpatient or outpatient setting, the medications Disulfiram (antabuse) or Naltrexone may be prescribed as one part of the treatment regimen.[112] When combined with alcohol, antabuse produces unpleasant physical effects, including headache, nausea, and anxiety. To ensure compliance with this aversive regimen, it is sometimes necessary to have a family member or significant other of the individual monitor daily ingestion. Naltrexone has effects very different from that of antabuse. Rather than induce illness, it blocks the pleasurable effects of alcohol by binding to relevant receptor sites in the central nervous system.

Some patients and treatment providers are very resistant to pharmacological treatment because they fear that it merely replaces one drug with another. It is important to recognize, however, that antabuse and Naltrexone do not have the same intoxicating effects as alcohol or other addictive drugs. Particularly in cases involving severe addiction, or those with severe psychosocial or medical complications, adjunctive pharmacotherapy may be very helpful, at least in the short run.

It is therefore advisable to seek consultation with a physician during the course of addiction treatment.

Historically, the content of addiction counseling focused on early life experiences and intrapsychic conflicts which were hypothesized to later result in addiction. However, empirical evidence has failed to identify common psychological conflicts or personality structures among alcoholics.[113] Therefore, more modern approaches focus to a greater extent on alcohol-specific cognitions rather than unconscious psychological forces. For example, the goal may be to correct illogical or maladaptive thoughts related to alcohol (e.g., "Whisky is my best friend.") or to correct dysfunctional attitudes about oneself in relation to drinking (e.g., "I'm a worthless person, so I might as well get drunk.").[114]

Behavioral strategies utilized in the treatment of alcoholism typically involve identifying "triggers" or "risk factors" for alcohol use and helping the person avoid these triggers. Therapy sessions may be spent practicing alcohol-refusal strategies and planning ways to minimize exposure to alcohol or alcohol-related stimuli. Group or family interventions may be particularly well-suited to developing and practicing these strategies.[115] Significant others, for example, are frequently reliable reporters about alcohol-related triggers and events. Similarly, in a group setting, the individual may learn about common triggers and coping strategies that have been identified or employed by other people.

By far the most common intervention for alcoholism is involvement in a self-help, "twelve-step" group such as Alcoholics Anonymous (AA). These programs generally focus on the goal of abstinence as opposed to reduced or controlled drinking.[116] Participants receive group support, repeated reminders about the consequences of alcohol use, and straightforward advice about methods for maintaining abstinence. AA is a spiritual (not necessarily religious) program that requires some belief in a power beyond oneself, and an acknowledgment of one's relative powerlessness over addiction in the absence of spiritual or communal support.

Although anecdotal testimonials to its effectiveness abound, the scientific evidence for the superiority of AA over other treatment approaches is largely lacking or contradictory.[117] Nevertheless, one of the most effective components of AA is the appointment of a "sponsor" for each participant, who is available to provide guidance and assistance 24 hours a day. Another advantage of AA is that, in many geographic regions, open group sessions are available without prior appointment most evenings of the week. Finally, AA uses a peer group approach to instill a number of psychologically healthy values, such as sincerity, forgiveness, tolerance, gratitude, humility, self-care, and affiliation.[118]

Not all people find the philosophy and structure of AA to be palatable. A common area of discomfort is the method for handling denial. At some point, AA participants are expected to publicly acknowledge their status as an alcoholic as well as their powerlessness over alcoholism as a necessary step towards recovery. Programs that are based more upon the Behavioral Model of addiction, in contrast, believe that such labeling is unnecessary and may even be counterproductive. Behavioral programs view alcoholism as a learned pattern, as opposed to a disease state to which one has unavoidably succumbed. Therefore, it is believed that acknowledging powerlessness over the disease may have the unintended consequence of making the person feel helpless about the future.

Some people find the group atmosphere of AA to be anxiety-provoking or discomforting. They may be fearful of speaking in front of other people, or they may not trust peers to exercise the same degree of discretion and confidentiality as licensed professionals. In contrast, others find group therapy to be the essential ingredient of successful treatment. In particular, it may be much more difficult to "con" or mislead other people who have "been there" themselves, and one might also expect to receive greater empathy and understanding from such persons.

As noted earlier, not all treatments are appropriate for all people. It is essential to find a good match between your own personal needs and the functional components of a particular program. Importantly, most programs share common core ingredients that appear to be essential for recovery. These include an opportunity to share feelings with others, to be heard, to be reinforced for abstinence, to reduce resistance in an atmosphere of trust, and to realize that you are not alone with the problem of alcoholism. Regardless of the specific program you choose, you are highly likely to receive some symptom relief simply by taking a measurable first step.

DEPRESSION: SYMPTOMS, CAUSES & TREATMENTS

If you are a lawyer who is suffering from depression, you are not alone. Several studies in the early 1990s have demonstrated that lawyers have among the highest rates of depression in the nation. For example, the North Carolina Bar Association[119] surveyed close to 2,600 attorneys and found that about 37% of them admitted to feeling depressed, approximately 25% reported physical symptoms of depression (e.g., appetite loss, lethargy), and over 11% reported suicidal ideation at least 1-2 times per month in the past year. A study[120] in the state of Washington surveyed 801 lawyers and found that 19% of them reported symptoms of clinical depression, a rate that was twice the national average for the general population. Finally, a Johns Hopkins University study[121] found that of 28 occupational groups across the country, lawyers were the most likely to suffer from depression and 3.6 times more likely than average.

THE SYMPTOMS

Depression is commonly felt across several experiential domains. The most characteristic emotional symptoms include sadness, fear of rejection and failure, guilt and anger. Mentally, a depressed person is likely to express a sense of pessimism and hopelessness, low self-esteem and helplessness; in more severe cases, depression is also characterized by suicidal ideation.

These thoughts and emotions often accompany some degree of cognitive impairment, such as an inability to think and concentrate, loss of memory, and an inability to "find the right words." Such symptoms can have a devastating effect on a lawyer's ability to work. Where attention to detail and logical analysis are crucial, mental impairment will usually reduce the speed and quality of the lawyer's work. There will be a greater likelihood of both administrative and substantive errors (e.g., failure to calendar, inadequate research), and that can lead to malpractice.

Depression is also characterized by a number of behavioral or physical symptoms, such as a sad facial appearance, crying, slowness of speech and movement, agitation, loss of appetite, sleep disorders, lowered interest in sexual activities, and various bodily complaints (e.g., stomach ache).

Current professional diagnostic methods presume that there are different types of depression, each of which have some distinctive features (e.g., intensity, duration). Many theorists also believe that the various depressions have distinct causes and require distinct treatments. Some symptoms of depression are symptoms of other ailments as well, both physical and psychological. For example, many of the behavioral/physical signs listed above can be indicative of alcoholism as well as depression. Indeed, alcoholism and depression often accompany each other.

Thus, especially in the more serious cases, it is recommended that proper diagnosis be sought from a qualified mental health professional. Oftentimes, a complete medical examination is recommended to rule out purely physical causes, such as viral infections, cerebral tumors, postpartum endocrine changes, or even medicinal side effects.

THE CAUSES

After many years of research, mental health professionals have reached a consensus on the symptoms of various types of depression, but not on their causes. There are those who believe depression is caused by genes or malfunctioning brain chemistry. Others think that environmental stressors and psychological habits are what cause depression.

As with all controversies of this type, there is a "chicken-or-egg" problem. Undoubtedly, depression involves both the mind and the body, but either one can cause the other. For example, it has been demonstrated that depression is both predictive of (cause) the onset of cardiovascular disease, as well as a common reaction to (effect) the onset of cardiovascular disease.[122] Thus, more and more experts are coming to the conclusion that there are various types of depression and that none of them can be explained by a single biological, biochemical, social, environmental or psychological factor. [123]

Obviously, some of the mental health problems lawyers experience have little to do with their vocation. On the other hand, the fact that lawyers experience higher rates of depression than average indicates that certain aspects of being an attorney must contribute to the problem. The most likely agent to explain the higher rates of depression among lawyers is "occupational stress," which is caused by the discrepancy between the "demands" of being a lawyer and the "capacity" of lawyers to manage such demands. This is magnified by the high level of perfectionism among lawyers. A complete discussion of what makes the practice of law so stressful is covered elsewhere in this book.

TREATMENT CHOICES

The majority of people with a depressive disorder do not seek professional help. This is sad in itself because depression happens to be a disorder that responds well to treatment in most cases. In severe instances of depression, such as when there is a high risk of suicide, hospitalization may be necessary. Generally, however, depressed patients are treated on an outpatient basis. Typically, treatment involves either psychotherapy, medications, or a combination of the two.

There are numerous schools of thought about how psychotherapy should be conducted with depressed patients. Some proponents of each approach claim that theirs is the best one. The truth is, that of the reputable psychotherapies, each has something valuable to offer, but none represents the ultimate answer. Here is a list of several types of psychotherapy:

Psychodynamic Psychotherapy - Sometimes referred to as "psychoanalytically oriented psychotherapy," the primary focus of this type of treatment is the examination of key relationships and experiences in a person's past and present, and how these are related to current problems. Change occurs through insight into previously unresolved conflicts and unconscious motives, which frees the person to make new choices.

Humanistic Psychotherapy - This type of treatment emphasizes the creation of a warm, supportive and non-judgmental therapeutic environment, in which the client feels free to engage in self-exploration and self-expression. It focuses on conscious thoughts and feelings, and current experiences. Change occurs because the positive therapeutic relationship encourages the client to experiment and grow.

Behavioral Therapy - This type of treatment applies learning principles to systematically transform a person's current self-destructive behaviors into adaptive behaviors. For example, a person who is prone to procrastination is taught concrete behavioral techniques to overcome this destructive habit. This brings about more positive or reinforcing real life experiences, which in turn leads to more optimistic thoughts and feelings.

Cognitive Psychotherapy - The aim of cognitive therapy is to correct dysfunctional thinking patterns. For example, people who are depressed tend to anticipate the worst and react to negative events by overgeneralizing and personalizing their effects. A cognitive therapist will attempt to make a client aware of and question the validity of these thought patterns, and consider alternative points of view.

Couple, Family and Group Psychotherapies - There are a variety of approaches that involve more than just one person in treatment. These approaches will differ somewhat as a function of the therapist's underlying theoretical points of view. What they share in common, however, is the idea that people grow through relating, learning from, getting support from and giving support to others.

Which type of psychotherapy should you choose? In numerous scientific studies,[124] cognitive therapy[125] has been shown to be particularly effective with depression. The approach is called "cognitive" in part because it requires clients to exercise logical reasoning in solving life's problems. Since lawyers are trained practitioners of rational analysis applied to practical problems, I find that this approach is an effective tool with them and have borrowed heavily from it in this book.

When seeking professional help, however, my advice is to look for a psychotherapist who appreciates the perspectives of several schools of thought, not just cognitive therapy. These other schools of thought have taught us a number of important lessons, including: the importance of helping patients understand how their current problems are often related to earlier life experiences; how helpful it is to examine and strengthen patients' personal relationships; that people do better with psychotherapists whom they perceive to be understanding, non-judgmental, caring and trustworthy; that modern medications for depression can be a useful tool as well.

Turning to the topic of medications, there are a number of highly effective anti-depressants available today. Among the latest is a type known as a serotonin-specific reuptake inhibitor. It helps restore the balance of serotonin in the brain, a neurotransmitter that has been found to affect moods. This type of medication is sold under such brand names as Prozac, Paxil, and Zoloft. An even newer type of medication that affects two neurotransmitters, serotonin and norepinephrine, is sold under the brand name of Effexor. These medications are both effective and have few side effects. It is best to have them prescribed and their effects monitored by a psychiatrist. Nevertheless, most family physicians are familiar with these drugs and commonly prescribe them in less severe cases of depression.

While there are times when all that is needed are medications, in general, they are most effective in combination with psychotherapy.[126] Medications take the edge off negative moods, help clarify thought processes, and increase patients' ability to participate in psychotherapy. What medications don't do is help people correct their core negative beliefs about themselves and the world, most of which have been learned over a lifetime of experiences. Changing such beliefs often requires more than just medications.

SELF-HELP FOR MILD DEPRESSION AND EXCESSIVE DRINKING

If your symptoms of depression or alcoholism are chronic or acute, the best advice I can give you is to seek help, either from a professional or a self-help organization. However, if your symptoms do not warrant outside intervention, there are a number of steps that you can take on your own. The fact that the rate of depression and alcoholism among lawyers is at least twice the national average, suggests that part of the problem is the stress that comes with the practice of law. Thus, one thing you can do to reduce your risk of getting depressed or developing a drinking problem, is apply the stress reduction techniques described in the other sections of this book. In addition, here are several other steps you can take.

DEALING WITH MILD DEPRESSION

The first thing to do when you are depressed is to improve your eating, drinking, exercise and sleep habits. These steps will help lift your sadness by affecting certain mood altering brain chemicals. Unfortunately, depressed people tend to do just the opposite; they disregard their diets, increase their alcohol or drug intake, stop exercising and don't adhere to a normal sleep schedule. You need to resist such urges.

Similarly, when you are depressed you need to pay particular attention to certain external or environmental factors that contribute to the way you feel. For example, depressed people tend to isolate themselves and become more idle. You need to do just the opposite. As much as possible, surround yourself with people you like and keep yourself busy. If you can't seem to do your important work effectively, do the less important work or even your chores. Make an effort to schedule experiences that will raise your spirits or cause you to laugh. You will be surprised how difficult it is to stay depressed under the influence of uplifting environmental forces.

Ultimately, however, you will need to confront the negative thoughts and emotions that are at the core of your depression. The first thoughts you may need to face are: "I can't do anything about my depression. Nothing will work." Ask yourself to only imagine doing some of the things that are recommended throughout this book. Then, ask yourself to try implementing just one or two of them. Once you shift from a passive to an active mode, and begin to actually work on solving your problems, you will find that some of your gloomy feelings may start to be replaced by glimmers of hope.

Depressed people often have a number of mental habits that are very dysfunctional. They tend to assume the worst, discount the positive, personalize events, blame themselves or others, overgeneralize and magnify things. These habits are embedded in statements like the following: " Unless I get a few more cases soon, this practice is doomed; people are not calling because I must not be that good." Thoughts like these need to be brought into conscious awareness, cross examined and revised, using the techniques outlined elsewhere in this book.

Another common trait among depressed people is that they tend to be perfectionistic about what they expect of themselves, what they think others expect of them, and what they expect of others.[127] Such expectations evoke a great many "should" statements, which in turn trigger guilt, fear of failure and fear of rejection. Using the techniques described elsewhere in this book, become aware of your perfectionistic thoughts and revise them. Strive for excellence, not perfection. Expect complications and recognize that the probability of your making errors is 100%. Adopt the attitude that there is no such thing as failure, only opportunities for improvement. Learn to measure your success by whether you are moving in the right direction, and not always by whether you have achieved your ultimate goal.

Since much of my advice here involves changing part of your personality, it could be one of the most difficult tasks you will ever undertake. For this reason, you may want to consider the possibility of seeking professional help. At the very least, you should refer to several other books that delve into the topic of depression in greater depth. Consider reading the following:

David D. Burns, Feeling Good: The New
Mood Therapy (1980)

David D. Burns, The Feeling Good
Handbook (1989)

Martin Seligman, Learned Optimism: The
Skill To Conquer Life's Obstacles,
Large And Small (1990).

Of course, you will find many other helpful books at your local library or bookstore.

DEALING WITH EXCESSIVE DRINKING

When it comes to excessive alcohol consumption, the first and best thing you can do for yourself is admit that you have a problem. Most people who drink too much simply deny it. If a little voice inside of you or someone who cares about you says that you are drinking too much, you probably are. There is an easy experiment that you can conduct to prove to yourself that you do not have a problem: stop all alcohol consumption for several weeks.

People who don't have a drinking problem, may find it inconvenient to abstain from alcohol for several weeks, but they are able to do it without much difficulty. If you can't abstain from drinking alcohol, find it difficult to do, or get irritated at the thought of it, then it is very likely that you do have a problem. Unless your condition is truly minimal, the best self-help advice I can offer you is to seek the aid of a professional or of a self-help group that specializes in this area. If yours is not a serious drinking problem, however, you can attempt to confront it yourself.

First, get a better understanding of why it is so difficult for you to abstain from alcohol. Determine the psychological role alcohol plays in your life, objectively measure the amount and frequency of your alcohol intake, and think about the negative effects that this has on you. Although it does take a little extra effort, you will get more insight into your drinking behaviors if you keep a daily diary of them. By way of further evaluating your drinking problem complete the following check list of alcohol dependency signs:

- ☐ Do you rely on alcoholic drinks to help you relax or be comfortable in social situations?
- ☐ Do you rely on alcoholic drinks to help you think better, be more creative, or work harder?
- ☐ Do you rely on alcoholic drinks to help you manage your moods, feel less depressed or tense, or forget your problems?
- ☐ Do you find yourself thinking about or having an urge to get an alcoholic drink at different times of the day?
- ☐ Do you often find yourself drinking more than others around you?

- ☐ Do you often experience regret about your drinking patterns?
- ☐ Do you find yourself lying or giving excuses about your alcohol intake?
- ☐ Do you often drink alone or hide liquor?
- ☐ Do you get intoxicated and have hangovers or memory blackouts?
- ☐ Is your drinking affecting your daily activities, such as being on time or getting your work done?

Once you have a better understanding of your drinking problem, try again to abstain from alcohol use for several weeks. Before doing so, know that all human experiences can be viewed as being composed of the following sequence of elements:

Stimulus > Thought > Emotion > Behavior

Since what you are trying to reduce is behavior, one way to proceed is to gain better control of the elements that precede it. For example, one thing you can do is get control of the stimuli or environmental factors that contribute to your drinking behaviors. This may include disposing of the liquor that you have at home or in the office, or refraining from going to places where liquor is readily available. You will find it much easier to reduce your drinking urges and behaviors when less liquor is available.

Similarly, you will need to get control of drink inducing thoughts and emotions that get triggered by external stimuli. Let us say that you have gone out to lunch with a client who orders a drink. When the waiter turns to you, you may find yourself thinking: "My client will be offended if I don't order. Besides, a drink will make me feel less anxious." These thoughts will trigger such emotions as fear of rejection and hope that tension will be reduced. The emotions will impel you to say: "I'll have a martini, please." If you learn to interrupt such thoughts and emotions and practice replacing them with healthier ones, your drinking patterns will change for the better. Using the methods of analysis described elsewhere in this book, you can systematically root out the thoughts and emotions that trigger your drinking behaviors.

Obviously, the information presented here is only introductory. Thus, I urge you to read other books that cover problem drinking in much greater depth. In particular, consider reading the following works:

Alcoholic Anonymous World Services, Twelve
Steps and Twelve Traditions (1990)

Albert Ellis & Emmett Velton, When AA
Doesn't Work For You: Rational Steps
To Quitting Alcohol (1992)

Stanton Peele & Archie Brodsky, The Truth
About Addiction and Recovery (1991)

Many other helpful books can be found in your local library or bookstore.

HOW TO GET HELP

If you are ready to reach out for help with your mental health or substance abuse problems, the organizations listed below will provide you with educational materials, lists of appropriate self-help groups, and referrals to mental health professionals. All of them are sensitive to your concerns regarding confidentiality. I recommend that you try their world wide web sites first, as they will provide you with much of the information you desire right on your computer screen and will link you to many other relevant resources.

LAWYER-SPECIFIC RESOURCES

In 1988, the American Bar Association created the Commission on Lawyer Assistance Programs (CoLAP; formerly known as the ABA Commission On Impaired Attorneys) and charged it with the task of educating the profession on both legal and treatment issues related to substance abuse and mental illness. In addition, the Commission has been supporting the development of lawyer assistance programs throughout the United States, Canada and Great Britain. It publishes a Directory of State and Local Lawyer Assistance Programs, educational materials, pamphlets, audiotapes and videotapes. For further information contact:

Commission On Lawyer Assistance Programs
American Bar Association
541 North Fairbanks Court, 14th Floor
Chicago, Illinois 60611-3314
Phone: (312) 988-5359; Fax: (312) 988-5280
World Wide Web: http://www.abanet.org/cia/home.html

In addition to contacting CoLAP (above), you can locate local organizations, self-help groups and professionals who provide helpful services to lawyers, by referring to your local legal directory, contacting you local bar association, or reading the relevant ads and articles in your local legal publications. Lawyer Assistance Programs (LAP) are now available in most localities. Their purpose is to help prevent and treat lawyer impairments through education and intervention oriented services. Most LAPs have toll-free hotlines. They take great care to protect the confidentiality of all communications and are an excellent resource for getting both legal and treatment information.

U.S. DEPARTMENT OF HEALTH & HUMAN SERVICES

A number of agencies under the U.S. Department of Health and Human Services can provide you with valuable information and advice regarding a wide range of mental health and substance abuse problems. Much of it is free for the asking. For further information contact:

National Institute of Mental Health (NIMH)
Public Inquiries - Rm. 7C-02
5600 Fishers Lane; Rockville, MD 20857
Phone: (301) 443-4513
World Wide Web: http://www. nimh.nih.gov/

The National Clearinghouse for Alcohol
and Drug Information (NCADI)
P.O. Box 2345; Rockville, MD 20847-2345
Phone: (800) 729-6686; Fax: (301) 468-6433
World Wide Web: http://www.health.org/index.htm

National Institute on Alcohol Abuse
and Alcoholism (NIAA)
6000 Executive Boulevard - Willco Building
Bethesda, MD 20892-7003
Phone: (800) 662-4357
World Wide Web: http://www.niaaa.nih.gov/

SELF-HELP GROUPS

Self-help groups are designed to empower people who
share similar concerns by bringing them together. They provide
emotional support, information and practical help. There are
self-help organizations for a wide range of problems, ranging
from alcoholism and depression to coronary disease, gambling,
debt and single parenting. Many groups have national offices
with local branches throughout the US. Local branches can be
found in your telephone directory, under the special section that
lists human services. Most self-help groups will mail you a free
set of informational materials with no questions asked. Here is a
list of several national organizations that will provide you with
useful information and a list of local self-help groups:

Alcoholics Anonymous (AA)
475 Riverside Drive, New York, NY 10115
Phone: (212) 870-3400; Fax: (212) 870-3003
World Wide Web: http://www.casti.com/aa/

International Lawyers in Alcoholics Anonymous (ILAA)
200 South Third, Las Vegas, NV 89155
Phone: (702) 455-4711; Fax: (702) 383-8465

Secular Organizations For Sobriety (SOS)
National Clearinghouse - Center for Inquiry
5521 Grosvenor Boulevard, Los Angeles, CA 90066
Phone: (310) 821-8430; Fax: (310) 821-2610
World Wide Web: http://www.codesh.org/sos/#whatis

National Mental Health Consumers'
Self-Help Clearinghouse
1211 Chestnut Street, Philadelphia, PA 19107
Phone: (800) 553-4539; Fax: (215) 636-6310
World Wide Web:
http:/www.libertynet.org/~mha/cl_house.html

PROFESSIONAL HELP

Finding a mental health professional is like finding a lawyer. Most people think that it is best to get a personal recommendation from a family member, friend or physician. Alternative methods include looking in the local telephone directory or seeking referrals from professional organizations, universities, and hospitals. In addition, there is the option of calling someone whose name appears in the media.

There are three basic types of mental health professionals: psychologists, psychiatrists and social workers. At times, each of these professions claims to have superiority in certain domains. For example, some psychiatrists claim that their ability to prescribe drugs as well as administer psychotherapy, makes them uniquely qualified to treat all mental illnesses. Some psychologists claim that their greater reliance on psychotherapy than on drugs and their special expertise in testing, makes them better diagnosticians and psychotherapists. In truth, however, such generalizations are simply not useful in finding someone to help you with your specific set of problems.

It is best to rely on the reputation of the particular professional rather than of his or her profession. Interview several mental health professionals before making a choice. The initial meeting, often granted at no cost, can help you establish the individual's credentials, experience, treatment preferences, and personality. Liking and trusting your provider is important in general health care, but it is critical in mental health care. Similarly, since much of the treatment will require your collaboration, the treatment strategy needs to make sense to you. Remember that it is possible for you to work with more than one provider. For example, a psychologist or social worker can act as your psychotherapist, while your family physician or psychiatrist monitors your medications.

SECTION VII

MANAGE

TIME

Unless we are careful, we tend to slip into an attitude toward time which is rather like that of a passenger who sits backward on a speeding train.

Robert Grudin

REMEDIES FOR TIME WASTERS

"I wasted time, and now doth time waste me."
William Shakespeare

The stress management techniques described in previous sections, instructing you to reconsider your own thoughts and emotions, can be applied to all areas of your life. Since time management is a primary concern for most lawyers,[128] I thought it would be useful to devote a few pages to it by way of illustration. My basic point throughout this section is this: Surface level time management advice, which gives you a list of "do's and don'ts," is simply ineffective for most people. Real change requires you to understand, evaluate and improve the thoughts and emotions that are at the core of why you use your time inefficiently.

In one of the best time management books ever written, entitled *The Time Trap*, Alec Mackenzie[129] identified the twenty biggest time wasters as follows:

1. Management by Crisis	11. Meetings
2. Telephone Interruptions	12. Paper Work
3. Inadequate Planning	13. Unfinished Tasks
4. Attempting Too Much	14. Inadequate Staff
5. Drop-in Visitors	15. Socializing
6. Ineffective Delegation	16. Confused Authority
7. Personal Disorganization	17. Poor Communication
8. Lack of Self-Discipline	18. Inadequate Controls
9. Inability to Say "No"	19. Incomplete Information
10. Procrastination	20. Travel

To boost your efficiency, you first need to identify your primary time wasting habits. The best way is to keep a precise two-week time log that will answer the age old question, "Where does my time go?" For each of ten working days, keep a diary of everything you do. Briefly describe each activity, note when it started, the total time it took, and whether it was important and/or urgent. (See the form provided at the end of this chapter.)

Once you have made a list of your time wasting habits, choose one or two that you think would be easiest to break. Try changing your behaviors and keep score of how well you do. The chances are that your bad habits will be more difficult to break than you thought. If that is the case, you will need to delve into the thoughts and emotions that drive your behaviors, as illustrated in previous sections of this book.

According to clients I have counseled, the following three time wasters are particularly troublesome for lawyers:

> interruptions
>> procrastination
>>> ineffective delegation

Allow me to illustrate how to handle each of these problems.

INTERRUPTIONS

It is very difficult to resist a ringing phone or a colleague who pops into your office and asks, "Got a minute?" Yet, these types of interruptions waste so much time that you must resist them. Not only does the interruption itself take you away from important work, but afterward there is a significant time-lag in regaining your previous level of concentration.

The usual advice given to solve this problem is very simple: Whenever possible, do not allow important work to be interrupted. Unfortunately, following this advice is not that easy. Although behavioral tips on reducing interruptions are the subject of many books[130] on time management, they are difficult to effectuate until you recognize the psychological changes you will need to make first. That is, people who cannot control interruptions commonly have unconscious motives that pull them in the opposite direction. Until you confront these motives, nothing will change.

For example, some people are reluctant to stop others from interrupting them because they are afraid of being offensive, and in turn of being rejected. In addition, there are those who allow themselves to be interrupted because they cannot stand the suspense of not knowing what other people want, and have a difficult time resisting the pull of curiosity. Interruptions make some of us feel important, and they help justify another major time waster, namely procrastination.

To uncover your hidden motives, try disallowing yourself to be interrupted a few times and record your resulting thoughts and emotions. Once you fully understand the psychological dynamics involved, try to evaluate their validity. For example, you might ask yourself: "Is it really true that if I don't respond to every interruption immediately, people will reject me?" After you recognize the illogic of your habitual thoughts and emotions, you can work on replacing them with more adaptive ones. Now, you will be in a position to implement the behavioral tips given by time management experts.

For example, in the case of telephone interruptions, it may require training a skilled secretarial assistant to say the right things: "I'm very sorry, but Ms. Smith is not available right now. However, may I make a telephone appointment at a time that she can call you back?" Most people say "yes," and this gives the attorney immediate control over the timing of the telephone conversation.

Prior to actually making the telephone appointment, the assistant should ask the caller: "May I tell Ms. Smith what this is about so that she can prepare herself prior to returning your call?" At this point, the assistant makes a determination as to whether the matter can be handled by someone else, including herself/himself. He or she might say something like: "I think that I can get that information for you out of the file. May I call you right back?" On the other hand, if the judgment is made that the matter requires the attorney's immediate attention, he/she might say: "Oh my! This sounds urgent. Let me see if I can interrupt/find Ms. Smith to see if she can call you as soon as possible. One of us will call you back in a few minutes."

If the matter requires the attorney's attention but is not urgent, the assistant can go ahead and make a telephone appointment during pre-designated blocks of time, preferably before lunch or toward the end of the day. These are times when people are least likely to stay on the phone any longer than necessary. Another strategy might be for you to designate times that tend to match your energy levels. For example, some people do their best writing in the morning, and phone calling later in the day.

Drop-in visitors can be handled with equal finesse. For example, after determining the nature of the issues to be discussed, you can say something like: "I really do want to talk to you about this and think that I can be of help. However, right now I must finish this work. Can we make an appointment, at a time when I can give you my full attention?" Then, when you make an appointment, schedule it at a time that meets your needs. It is also a good idea to set up several meetings in a row, one after the other, so that each has a set time limit and is not likely to go on for too long.

Nothing I have suggested is meant to imply that you be unresponsive to your clients or colleagues. In fact, lack of attention is the single biggest complaint that clients have about lawyers, and their number one reason for changing lawyers. From a client's perspective, there is nothing more frustrating than a lawyer who does not return phone calls. That is *not* what I am recommending. My message is that you should get greater control of when you attend to phone calls and visitors.

PROCRASTINATION

Procrastination is such a common habit that some people have actually come to consider it as an adaptive trait. (A few lawyers I know think of it as an art form.) This faulty logic is expressed when some of us say, "I work better under pressure." In reality, it would be more accurate to say: " I work more efficiently when I don't procrastinate. Unfortunately, that usually happens when time has run out and I have no choice but to stop procrastinating. I wish I could stop procrastinating when I am not under pressure."

Do you see the difference? By definition, you work more efficiently and think more clearly when you do not procrastinate. Time pressure does not improve your performance; it simply forces you to stop procrastinating. Your peak performance, however, is likely to occur when you do not procrastinate and are *not* under time pressure as well. Not only is this preferable for health reasons, but it is also more likely to prevent mental errors and increase creativity.

As with the other time-wasters, procrastination has underlying psychological causes. Generally, the reason we avoid something is that we think it will lead to emotional pain. A common emotion procrastination avoids is fear of failure. For example, a typical scenario might proceed as follows: You look at a file and say to yourself, "This is a difficult case." The underlying implication is that you are going to fail, and that triggers fear. Instead of confronting your original premise and all of its corollaries (e.g., "I'm not a good lawyer."), you get rid of the emotional pain by avoiding the task.

Another common reason people procrastinate is out of a genuine lack of interest in the work. You say to yourself, "This is going to be boring!" In turn, this leads to thoughts about your whole identity and whether your life is fulfilling. Such thoughts may trigger a variety of emotions, including anger, frustration and guilt. Again, instead of confronting your thoughts and emotions in a constructive manner, you reduce the emotional pain by simply avoiding the boring task.

Again, I urge you to discover the specific sets of thoughts and emotions that cause you to procrastinate. Having done so, confront them directly. Ask yourself solution/future oriented questions such as, "What can I do to resolve this issue once and for all?"

When you understand and begin to deal with the psychological issues that underlie procrastination, there are a number of behavioral tips you can follow. The most effective step you can take is to break projects down to smaller units. No matter how overwhelming a task may seem, you need to get your mind to view it as being composed of small and very doable steps. If you still find it threatening, break the task down to even smaller and smaller steps, until you can honestly say, "Individually each of these steps are very doable and painless." Then take each step in turn, spreading them out as much as is necessary. Having done this exercise a few times, you will find that it becomes easier and easier to procrastinate less and less.

INEFFECTIVE DELEGATION

Do you live by the rule that the way to get things done right is to do them yourself? Does everything your staff produces have to be reviewed by you? Do you get accused of being too perfectionistic, critical and controlling? If your answer to any of these questions is "yes," it is likely that you are an ineffective delegator.

An inability to effectively delegate work can be a most debilitating and time wasting habit. It means that you cannot maximize your achievement through the efforts of others, which in turn means that you are limiting the extent to which you can leverage your talents. In short, you will find it difficult to manage other people and are doomed to being a worker bee. That is, you are more likely to work longer hours and less likely to earn the higher levels of income.

Once more, the underlying causes of this disability are psychological. They include perfectionism (fear of mistakes), excessive feeling of responsibility for everything, lack of confidence in others, need for control and fear of being controlled, fear of competition from employees, etc. As with the other time wasters, you need to develop an understanding of the thoughts and emotions that prevent you from being an effective delegator. Then, evaluate their validity and replace them with thoughts and emotions that are more adaptive.

There are a number of books on the market that can teach you how to delegate.[131] The main thing you need to change is the belief that for things to be done right you have to do them yourself. Learn to live by a different rule: anything that can be done by others should be done by others. Of course, you must hire the right people, be clear in your instructions, and create a supportive psychological environment.

Effective managers accept the fact that everyone is imperfect and capable of making mistakes. They create an atmosphere in which mistakes are expected. Thus, they build the possibility of mistakes into their scheduling and develop procedures that filter them out without penalizing staff members. Staff are expected to grow and learn from their mistakes.

The effective manager provides moral support, coaches, and teaches the staff, but does not do its work. People are entrusted to continuously learn and improve. When staff members realize achievements and advance their status, the effective manager does not feel jealous or fearful, but rejoices in how well it reflects on his or her department.

TIME LOG FOR _____(DATE)

DESCRIBE ACTIVITY (e.g., phone with Tom, dictated brief, coffee & read newspaper)	START TIME (e.g., 9:30am)	ELAPSED TIME (e.g., 10 minutes)	IMPORTANT (I) vs. NOT IMPORT. (NI) -------------- URGENT (U) vs. NOT URGENT (NU)
END OF DAY REFLECTIONS (e.g., name big time wasters, give yourself suggestions)			

DO THE IMPORTANT THINGS FIRST

Most people get into the office and say to themselves: "First, let me clean up some (less important) loose ends. Then, when my desk is clear, I'll be able to concentrate on the more important things." Of course, all tasks take more time than expected, and there are always additional unanticipated projects that arise as well. By the end of the day, there is a realization that the important matters will have to wait until the next day. This scenario repeats itself many times until the important things become so urgent that they must get done first.

How can we put an end to this stressful style of working? Experts agree[132] that the most significant time management step any of us can take is to habitually *do the important things first.* This strategy is most fully explored in a book by Stephen Covey and two colleagues, entitled *First Things First.*[133] The authors point out that effective time managers symbolically keep their eye on two instruments: a compass and a clock. That is, they monitor their direction in life as well as their speed.

To do this, effective time managers learn to categorize all activities along two dimensions: *importance and urgency.* Furthermore, they try to fill their days with activities that are *important but not urgent.* This includes pursuits that involve long term planning, creativity and crisis prevention. One reason so many lawyers experience stress is that too often their days are absorbed by activities that are urgent. Although some urgent activities in law are inevitable, many of them are caused by procrastination, ineffective delegation, telephone interruptions, unnecessary meetings and other time-wasters. The key is to prevent important things from becoming urgent by finding ways of doing them first.

The adage, "first things first", is easy to comprehend, but difficult to follow. To start with, it requires us to know what is important. How many of us truly know what is important? Even when we do, how many of us march to our own drumbeat? When I discuss this issue with my clients, I often encounter strong resistance. Some lawyers actually tell me that they are too busy to figure out what is important. In reality, most of them are afraid to face some unpleasant truths, such as that they are not truly focusing on what is important in their lives.

Once you clarify what is important and do as many important things as are possible every single day, your life will change in a profound way. The immediate effect will be a great sense of satisfaction that results from living the life you want to lead and accomplishing the things that matter. Later, in the autumn of your life, as you sit in a rocking chair and ponder what it was all about, you will have few regrets.

THE CURE FOR OVERWORK

At the risk of offending some readers, I want to state emphatically that there is only one prescription for too much work: it is called *less work*. Right about now, you may be saying to yourself, "Simplification is fine up to a point, but this is ridiculous!" Nevertheless, I find it necessary to state the obvious because many intelligent people imagine that there are experts who can help them overcome the natural laws that govern time and space.

For example, a common recommendation given to overloaded lawyers is to seek time management advice. The problem, however, is that most time management strategies are designed to make people work more efficiently, not to work less. Generally, better time management is only temporarily effective. Armed with greater skill for efficiency, the typical workaholic lawyer, working in a workaholic law firm, soon takes on more tasks than ever and ends up just as stressed as ever. It is like consolidating your loans; the temporary effect is to reduce payments, but it usually does little to change spending habits. Many of us know this at an intuitive level and resist becoming good time managers. We anticipate that our only reward will be even more work.

Another common recommendation given to overburdened lawyers is to spend more time getting involved in alternative activities, such as pro bono work or community service. These activities do add variety to an attorney's day and they promote philanthropy and compassion, all of which are important. What they don't do, however, is reduce lawyers' workloads. For example, pro bono cases are as stressful and can take as much time as other cases. Similarly, community service does not give lawyers more personal time.

Of all the recommendations offered, the only ones that will give attorneys more personal time are for law firms to reduce their billable or working hour requirements and offer part-time and flextime opportunities. Although supporters of such recommendations offer arguments to allay economic concerns, let's face it: their implementation costs money. Senior partners are asked to consider more flexible working hours on the basis that such a policy will actually increase productivity or at least not hurt it, and that it will promote more effective recruitment and less turnover. Even if these assertions are true, however, a reduced number of working hours has to result in a reduced income for someone. At the very least, it will mean an income reduction for those who work fewer hours.

Thus, real change will require you to undergo a major reexamination of your basic values. The fact is that workaholism does speed up professional advancement and does result in greater income. What it does not do is allow you to reinforce close social and family bonds, or give you the time to engage in personal self-discovery. Both of these are necessary for a balanced and contented life.

Beware of remedies that sound easy. Restructuring life's major priorities is difficult. Money is a powerful motivator, especially when it is linked to psychological needs such as security, esteem, power, autonomy and love. Untangling these thorny connections and replacing them with a healthier balance of values is intricate work. Even the help of a psychotherapist does not guarantee success. In order to fit treatment into their schedules, workaholic lawyers tend to choose workaholic therapists. Generally, this is not a good match.

The kind of change that is required often involves delving into one's core and breaking through much denial, resistance, shame, fear and social pressure. It is not an easy process and requires a great deal of courage, but the goal is worthwhile.

QUANTITATIVELY SPEAKING

Imagine what it would mean if you could gain one extra hour per day- just one! That is, suppose that you could work more efficiently, so as to be finished one hour earlier each day. The cumulative effect on your productivity would be astounding. For example, assuming that you work a modest 5 days a week for 48 weeks of the year, you would have an additional:

- 5 hours per week
- 20 hours per month
- 6 forty-hour weeks per year
- 1 year every 9 years

To achieve these gains, all you need to do is waste less time. Since most of us do not work very efficiently, this is not difficult to accomplish. To prove the point, think about the last time you were going on vacation or were up against a major deadline. Did you work more efficiently than usual? You probably planned your days better, shaved a few minutes off of each conversation, procrastinated less, etc. Without going overboard, you can do the same every working day.

Most of us imagine that once we acquire extra time we will become more productive and successful in both our professional and personal lives. Having the extra time certainly makes it more possible for you to achieve additional professional goals, seek personal adventures, express your creativity, contribute to your community, and relate better to your family and friends. However, it is naive to assume that you will automatically use your extra time wisely. How you use your extra time is a separate challenge.

QUALITATIVELY SPEAKING

Prior to becoming more efficient with your time, analyze what the term "time management" means to you. One point to consider is that we can no more manage the passage of time as measured by a clock, than we can command the sun to rise. Unlike many other resources in life, we cannot store time or determine when it shall or shall not be used. Here on earth anyway, time ticks away at the same speed regardless of our activities. However, we do have the ability to manage our psychological experiences of time. That is, time can be made to feel shorter or longer as a function of our activities. Thus, the term "time management" really relates to how we manage ourselves, not time - what makes us tick, not the clock.

Most people think about time management in quantitative terms: "doing things faster or getting more things done." However, time management can have a qualitative meaning as well: "doing things that truly matter or that you enjoy." With this distinction in mind, think about who is the better time manager. Is it the person who spends time on endeavors that are enjoyable and meaningful, or the person who is efficient and can do a great many tasks? Although these are not mutually exclusive options, pitting them against each other may lead to several insights about the kind of time manager you really want to become.

Once you begin thinking of time management in both quantitative and qualitative terms, everything you do will take on new meaning. You will think about what your calendar truly represents: a diary of how you are choosing to spend your life. The number of things you accomplish will be weighed against their importance and meaningfulness. The results or products of your efforts will be evaluated in the context of the extent to which you enjoyed the process. (Time will become such a precious commodity that if your current job does not allow you to even think about such matters, you may need to consider a change.)

To become an effective time manager, the first thing you should do is explain to yourself why you want to manage your time more effectively in the first place. Take out a sheet of paper and list your goals. Start with the most abstract goals (e.g., self-esteem, love, security, adventure, creativity) and proceed to the most concrete (e.g., argue before the Supreme Court, more time with kids, earn $200K per year, travel to the Orient).

Without a set of strong motives, your attempts at time management will fail. You might try a few techniques and temporarily improve your productivity. However, unless this leads to greater job or life satisfaction, you will become less and less motivated to use them. To succeed, you must be clear about the personal and professional improvements that time management will help you achieve.

SECTION VIII

EPILOGUE: SKILLS FOR SUCCESS

To laugh often and much; to win the respect of intelligent people and the affection of children; to earn the appreciation of honest critics and endure the betrayal of false friends; to appreciate beauty; to find the best in others; to leave the world a bit better, whether by a healthy child, a garden patch or a redeemed social condition; to know even one life has breathed easier because you have lived. This is to have succeeded.

Anonymous[134]

FOUR STEPS TO SUCCESS

My definition of a successful lawyer is a person who finds happiness and does not experience chronic distress. Successful lawyers, like successful people from all walks of life, have habitual ways of thinking, emoting, and behaving. They:

1. Set Goals
2. Develop Plans
3. Act
4. Continuously Improve

Successful lawyers know that most things are created twice, once in the mind and once in reality. Thus, one of the things they have in common is a set of clear and concrete goals that are free of mixed emotions.

Knowing what they want, they also develop concrete plans to fulfill their goals. These plans are then broken down into small steps that are achievable and do not appear overwhelming. They try to build fun into their plans because pleasurable tasks are more likely to get done and bring greater satisfaction.

Successful lawyers act on their plans. It isn't that they do not experience fear, it is just that they are courageous enough to accept themselves as fallible. They recognize that the probability of everything going exactly according to plan is almost zero. Thus, they constantly seek feedback and make adjustments. For them there is no such thing as failure, only opportunities for growth and improvement.

Finally, successful lawyers emulate other successful lawyers in taking these steps. I urge you to do the same.

STRIVE FOR EXCELLENCE
NOT PERFECTION

Having observed the high levels of stress and failure that aiming for perfection induces, I have come to the conclusion that "excellence" is a far superior goal. Upon hearing this, clients often ask me: "Aren't you just playing with words? Isn't excellence a synonym for perfection? If there is a difference between these two concepts, are you suggesting that I lower my standards?" My response to all three questions is "No.".

By definition, perfectionists try to be flawless. To accomplish their goal, they strive to avoid all errors. In part, they hope to produce perfect work products so that they can experience the pleasure of not feeling the fear and guilt associated with making mistakes. For example, consider the following excerpt from a commencement address given to the graduates of the University of Arkansas Law School in 1993:

> The reputation you develop for intellectual and ethical integrity will be your greatest asset or your worst enemy....Treat every pleading, every brief, every contract, every letter, every daily task as if your career will be judged on it.... I cannot make this point to you too strongly. There is no victory, no advantage, no fee, no favor which is worth even a blemish on your reputation for intellect and integrity....Dents to the reputation in the legal profession are irreparable. [135]

At first, these words sound like good advice coming from someone who takes pride in his or her work and who values integrity. A closer look, however, reveals a principle that may be too extreme. The speaker advised the graduates to strive for perfection rather than excellence. This point becomes more evident when one realizes that the speaker was Vincent Foster, a very successful attorney who became President Clinton's deputy counsel in 1993. The excerpted speech was given just a few months prior to his tragic suicide.

What makes the goal of achieving perfection so unhealthy is its intolerance of human error. Since perfection does not exist, perfectionists are doomed to be perpetually frustrated. Their fear of mistakes tends to diminish their job satisfaction, makes them defensive and can lead to depression. Paradoxically, eventually this reduces the quality of their work. Thus, perfection is a very costly illusion.

Whereas perfection is an absolute measure, excellence is a relative one. For example, both the work of a first grader and that of a law student can be excellent without being equivalent. Neither can be perfect, however. Thus, by definition, excellence does not require perfection and is achievable. Given these distinctions, choosing to strive for excellence rather than perfection has important implications for how much job satisfaction you derive and how successful you become.

People who strive for excellence accept themselves as imperfect beings who produce imperfect products. This is not a failure, just a reality. Their acceptance of the fact that there are always better ways of doing things, makes them less fearful of making mistakes. This allows them to constantly grow and improve. Each new learning experience may remind them of their imperfections and even trigger some guilt. However, such thoughts and emotions are quickly replaced by the pride and joy that comes with getting better and better at something. For this reason, they tend to get more pleasure and satisfaction out of their work than perfectionists. In addition, because they are so much more open to feedback and continuous growth, their work products are often of higher quality than those of perfectionists.

PERSONALITIES OF STRESS RESISTANT LAWYERS

Even though stress generally results in higher rates of mental and physical illnesses, not all people react the same way to their environment. There are people who have physiological and psychological dispositions that make them more resistant than others to the effects of daily strains. Coincidentally, several studies of lawyers have uncovered what some of these psychological dispositions might be.[136] Although the primary purpose of these studies was to study stress resistance in general, and not lawyers in particular, they give us insight into the personality traits that tend to differentiate the healthy from the unhealthy lawyer.

COMMITMENT

One of the characteristics that has been found to distinguish lawyers who don't feel as much of the strain that comes with the practice of law is a sense of commitment to oneself, work, family and community. Committed lawyers believe in the truth, importance and interest value of their professional and personal activities. They think that what they do on a daily basis is both meaningful and relevant. This inner sense of purpose makes them more immune to external disappointments.

Committed lawyers are also more likely to be involved in the world around them. As a result, they have more meaningful relationships with other people, including colleagues, family, friends and members of their community. This makes them even more immune to external stresses in that they are more likely to have the comfort of knowing that they can rely on other people for support.

COMPETENCE

Another trait that distinguishes lawyers who feel less stressed by the practice of law is a sense of being a competent person. Such lawyers do not believe in fate as much as in their own ability to influence the world. They perceive life's stresses as predictable consequences of logical events, and themselves as capable of controlling or at least influencing such events.

Rather than chronically complaining about their problems, competent lawyers focus on finding solutions to them. They analyze the past, but only en route to thinking about the future and how to improve it. They confront their problems rather than run from them.

For example, when stressed, competent lawyers will choose to improve their eating, drinking and exercise habits, rather than the other way around, knowing that better physical health is part of what it takes to get through tough times. Instead of taking time off, they become more actively involved in dealing with their underlying problems.

GOOD WILL

In a recent study, it was found that cynicism, chronic anger and aggressive behavior are highly predictive of heart disease and mortality rates among lawyers.[137] Healthy lawyers are characterized by the opposite traits, such as trust, good will and friendliness. They have a generally positive view of humankind, and treat others with kindness and respect.

Healthy lawyers act out of their own sense of integrity and expect others to act accordingly. When others don't meet their expectations, healthy lawyers tend to be less perfectionistic and more forgiving of other people's failures. Similarly, they tend to be more forgiving of themselves. They don't get overly disappointed when things don't go their way.

Because of their greater sense of inner calm, healthy lawyers have fewer tantrums. They seldom throw things, slam doors, hang up the telephone on people, engage in name calling or blaming. This does not preclude them from being assertive, however. They are clear about their objectives and use all legal and ethical means to achieve them. They just don't get angry as often and try not to be affected by the hostility of others.

HOW DO I BECOME ONE?

Note that the studies to which I have referred are correlational. That is, all we know is that stress resistant lawyers tend to be more committed to what they do, feel more capable of controlling their lives, and are kinder and gentler to themselves and others. We don't know for sure whether these traits cause less stress or are simply symptoms of it. We don't know whether the aforementioned psychological traits are caused by underlying genetic factors.

Even though stress experts argue about such things, most agree that in the absence of real proof to the contrary it is a good idea to make the kind of changes in one's personality that are associated with low stress. Even if you do have certain genetic predispositions, all personality traits are modifiable to some degree. Thus, you do have the power to change.

ALL THE SAGES AGREE

In my writings and seminars, I try very hard to come up with new ideas and insights on how to achieve success in life. Repeatedly, however, I find that the fundamental keys to success are not new. Parents, teachers, religious leaders and many others have all said the same things over and over again. Their advice is usually very simple to understand, but difficult to implement. None of them offer quick-fix solutions.

David G. Myers[138] reviewed thousands of psychological studies on what makes people happy in a book entitled *The Pursuit of Happiness*. He found that certain ideas about happiness are myths. For example, it is not true that few people are happy or that wealth leads to happiness. Not surprisingly, he also found that the following do make people happy:

- physical health and fitness
- reasonable goals and expectations
- positive self-esteem and optimism
- feelings of competence and control
- challenging work balanced by leisure
- meaningful relationships and intimacy
- contributing to a community
- a good marriage and family

In another book entitled *The 7 Habits of Highly Effective People*, Stephen R. Covey[139] outlined the fundamental keys to success that his exhaustive review of the literature revealed. He defined *effective people* as individuals who actualize their potential. According to Covey, effective people tend to develop a common set of internalized principles and patterns of behavior that are summarized in the following list:

- Be Proactive
- Begin With The End In Mind
- Put First Things First
- Think Win/Win
- Seek First To Understand,
          Then To Be Understood
- Synergize
- Sharpen The Saw

To be proactive means to take responsibility for your own life. It is the opposite of being reactive, of allowing or depending on other people and circumstances to determine your success. It means taking the initiative and being future oriented.

To begin with the end in mind means to have a clear set of goals that are based on what you truly value. One way to get a glimpse of your basic values is to imagine yourself at the end of your life, reflecting on your own achievements: What will you want to have accomplished?

Putting first things first is a core time management skill. It means putting your efforts into things that are important to you. In addition, it means working on important things far enough in advance so as to not make them urgent and laden with pressure.

Thinking win/win means seeking solutions that are mutually beneficial to all parties. Given the adversarial nature of our legal system, it is natural to conclude that this principle may not apply to lawyers. Covey would disagree, however. He would argue that the win/win principle applies to all negotiations, and that lawyers negotiate far more frequently than they litigate. In fact, litigation occurs mostly when people are unable or unwilling to find a win/win solution to their disputes.

Certainly, it makes sense to believe that long term relationships succeed more often when they are based on a win/win principle. For this reason, it is an effective principle for lawyers to follow in negotiating agreements that involve ongoing relationships (e.g., partnerships, child custody). Eventually, win/lose agreements go sour and when that happens, lawyers on both ends get the blame. Thus, Covey would say that rather than being idealistic, a lawyer who thinks win/win is likely to be more successful in the long run.

Seeking first to understand and only then to be understood, is a powerful communication habit. It means listening before talking, evaluating before acting, and empathizing with the concerns of others before attempting to mitigate your own. People are much more positively predisposed to the concerns of others once their own are understood.

To synergize means to activate all of your other "habits" in such a harmonious fashion so as to get an enhanced combined effect. One such effect is the uncanny ability that some people have of solving seemingly insolvable problems. What they do is suspend their preconceptions, give up their defensive postures, focus on creating solutions, and solicit alternative perspectives.

Finally, Covey suggests that effective people are committed to continuous improvement. They take time to renew themselves mentally, physically, emotionally, socially and spiritually, through such activities as continuing education, re-evaluation of goals, community service, exercise, and relaxation.

They may use different words, but all of the sages of our culture agree. There are certain truths about success that are simply self-evident. The sooner you accept these truths, the sooner you will find your own slice of happiness.

THE THINGS I HAVE LEARNED - SO FAR

I was lucky growing up. Although neither of my parents took a single course on the psychology of success, they taught me important lessons about it. Whenever I brooded over making a mistake, my father would say: "I am glad you have the courage to admit your error, but the important thing for you to think about now is what have you have learned and what you are going to do the next time." Similarly, when I felt sad about how difficult life is sometimes, my mother would say: "Meaning comes from within. You have the ability to create beauty or ugliness, happiness or unhappiness. It's up to you."

Experience has taught me an additional lesson: Usually, there are no shortcuts! I don't mean to suggest that the difficult paths we choose for ourselves are always desirable. Indeed, I have often gone in the wrong direction altogether or made things much more tedious than necessary. I just mean that whenever I have overcome important challenges, they have generally required a great deal of effort, perseverance, patience, and courage. Normally, the shortcuts I have attempted have only lead me to dead-ends.

Another meaningful lesson I have learned is that life should be a continuous growth experience. For example, I realize that this book is incomplete and has imperfections, for it reflects only the things I have learned so far. However, this edition is better than the last one. Furthermore, I plan to continue studying the legal profession and refining my recommendations. It is my hope that you too will consider the stress management techniques you have learned from this book as only one step in your efforts to continuously improve your life. If you do that, then both of us will have truly succeeded.

ENDNOTES

[1]American Bar Association, At The Breaking Point: The Report Of A National Conference On The Emerging Crisis In The Quality Of Lawyers' Health And Lives, And Its Impact On Law Firms And Client Services (1991); American Bar Association, The State Of The Legal Profession - 1984: Report Of The Young Lawyers Division (1985); American Bar Association, The State Of The Legal Profession - 1990: Report Of The Young Lawyers Division (1991); American Bar Association, ABA Young Lawyers Division Survey: Career Satisfaction (1995); North Carolina Bar Association, Quality Of Life Survey Of North Carolina Attorneys: Report Of Quality Of Life Task Force (1991).

[2]D. L. Arron, Running From The Law: Why Good Lawyers Are Getting Out Of The Legal Profession (1991); W. Bachman, Law V. Life: What Lawyers Are Afraid To Say About The Legal Profession (1995); D. Margolick, *Alienated Lawyers Seeking-And Getting-Counsel In Making The Transition To Other Careers,* N.Y. Times B7 (Feb. 10, 1989).

[3]G.A.H. Benjamin, E.J. Darling & B.D. Sales, *The Prevalence of Depression, Alcohol Abuse, And Cocaine Abuse Among United States Lawyers,* 13 International Journal of Law and Psychiatry 233 (1990); W.W. Eaton, J.C. Anthony, W. Mandel & R. Garrison, *Occupations And The Prevalence Of Major Depressive Disorder,* 32 Journal Of Occupational Medicine 1079 (1990): A. Elwork & G.A.H. Benjamin, *Lawyers In Distress,* 23 The Journal Of Psychiatry And Law 205 (1995).

[4] See, J.W. Santrock, A.M. Minnett & B.D. Campbell, The Authoritative Guide To Self-Help Books (1994).

[5] American Bar Association, At The Breaking Point: The Report Of A National Conference On The Emerging Crisis In The Quality Of Lawyers' Health And Lives, And Its Impact On Law Firms And Client Services (1991).

[6] American Bar Association, The State Of The Legal Profession - 1984: Report Of The Young Lawyers Division (1985).

[7] American Bar Association, The State Of The Legal Profession - 1990: Report Of The Young Lawyers Division (1991).

[8] L. R. Richard, Psychological Type And Job Satisfaction Among Practicing Lawyers In The United States (1994; Ph.D. dissertation, Temple University, Philadelphia, available through University Microfilms International Dissertation Services.)

[9] North Carolina Bar Association, Quality of Life Survey of North Carolina Attorneys: Report of Quality of Life Task Force (1991).

[10] G.A.H. Benjamin, A. Kaszniak, B.D. Sales & S.B. Shanfield, *The Role Of Legal Education In Producing Psychological Distress Among Law*

Students And Lawyers, American Bar Foundation Research Journal 225 (1986).

[11] G.A.H. Benjamin, E.J. Darling & B.D. Sales, *The Prevalence of Depression, Alcohol Abuse, And Cocaine Abuse Among United States Lawyers,* 13 International Journal of Law and Psychiatry 233 (1990).

[12] W.W. Eaton, J.C. Anthony, W. Mandel & R. Garrison, *Occupations And The Prevalence Of Major Depressive Disorder,* 32 Journal Of Occupational Medicine 1079 (1990).

[13] A. Elwork & G.A.H. Benjamin, *Lawyers In Distress,* 23 The Journal of Psychiatry and Law 205 (1995).

[14] C. L. Cooper, Handbook Of Stress, Medicine, And Health (1995); S. E. Taylor, Health Psychology (1995).

[15] R. Klein, *The Relationship Of The Court And Defense Counsel: The Impact On Competent Representation And Proposals For Reform,* 29(3) Boston College Law Review 531 (1988).

[16] ABA Commission On Impaired Attorneys, An Overview Of Lawyer Assistance Programs In The United States 1 (1991); C.P. Anderson, Survey Regarding Impairment and Attorney Misconduct in Illinois (1993) (unpublished statistics available through the Attorney Registration and Disciplinary Commission of the Supreme Court of Illinois); M.R. Ramos, *Legal Malpractice: The Profession's Dirty Little Secret,* 47 Vanderbilt Law Review 1657, 1698 (1994); Standing Committee On Lawyers' Professional Liability, The Lawyer's Desk Guide To Legal Malpractice 105 (1992);

[17] D. E. Conner, *Depressed Employees Get Big ADA Awards,* Lawyers Weekly USA, A1 (Sept. 25, 1995); *Reasonable Accommodation,* 14 (9) Mental Health Law Reporter 65 (September, 1996).

[18] D. Margolick, *Alienated Lawyers Seeking-And Getting-Counsel In Making The Transition To Other Careers,* New York Times B7 (Feb.10, 1989). M.R. Ramos, *Legal Malpractice: The Profession's Dirty Little Secret,* 47 Vanderbilt Law Review 1657, 1715 (1994).

[19] M.R. Ramos, *Legal Malpractice: The Profession's Dirty Little Secret,* 47 Vanderbilt Law Review 1657 (1994).

[20] Mary Ann Glendon, A Nation Under Lawyers 15 (1994).

[21] The conclusions in this chapter are based on a review of the following literature: American Bar Association, The State Of The Legal Profession - 1990: Report Of The Young Lawyers Division (1991); M.A. Altman, Life After Law (1991); J.C. Barefoot, K.A. Dodge, B.L. Peterson, W.G. Dahlstrom & R.B. Williams, *The Cook-Medley Hostility Scale: Item Content And Ability To Predict Survival,* 51 Psychosomatic Medicine 46 (1989); G.A.H. Benjamin, A. Kaszniak, B.D. Sales & S.B. Shanfield, *The Role Of Legal Education In Producing Psychological Distress Among Law Students And Lawyers,* American Bar Foundation Research Journal 225

(1986); D.L. Arron, Running from the law: Why good lawyers are getting out of the legal profession (1991); S. Benson, *Why I Quit Practicing Law*, Newsweek, November 4, 1991, at 10; Commission on Women in the Profession (ABA), Lawyers and Balanced Lives: A Guide to Drafting and Implementing workplace policies for Lawyers (1990); M.C. Fisk, *A Measure Of Satisfaction*, 12(38) The National Law Journal, S2-S12 (1990); R. Frances, G. Alexopoulos, & V. Yandow, *Lawyers' Alcoholism*, 4(2) Advances In Alcohol And Substance Abuse 59 (1984); E.H. Friedman & H.K. Hellerstein, *Occupational Stress, Law School Hierarchy And Coronary Artery Disease In Cleveland Attorneys*, 36 Psychosomatic Medicine 72 (1968); S. Goldberg, *Satisfaction*, 75(4) ABA Journal 40 (1989); B.S. Gould, *Beyond Burnout*, 10(3) Barrister 4 (1983); E.H. Greenebaum, *Lawyers' Relationship To Their Work*, 53 Legal Education 651 (1978); M.D. Gupta, *Machiavellianism Of Different Occupational Groups*, 18(2) Indian Journal of Psychometry and Education 61 (1987); R.L. Hirsch, *Will Women Leave The Law*, 16(1) Barrister 22 (1989); R.L. Hirsch, *Are You On Target?*, 12(1) Barrister 17 (1985); J.P. Heinz & E.O. Laumann, Chicago Lawyers: The Social Structure of the Bar (1984); S.E. Jackson, J.A. Turner & A.P. Brief, *Correlates Of Burnout Among Public Service Lawyers*, 8(4) Journal of Occupational Behavior 339 (1987); S.C. Kobasa, *Commitment And Coping In Stress Resistance Among Lawyers*, 42(4) Journal of Personality and Social Psychology 707 (1982); L.J. Landwehr, *Lawyers As Social Progressives Or Reactionaries: The Law And Order Cognitive Orientation Of Lawyers*, 7 Law And Psychology Review 39 (1982); G.W. LaRussa, *Portia's Decision: Women's Motives For Studying Law And Their Later Career Satisfaction As Attorneys*, 1 Psychology of Women Quarterly 350 (1977); J.S. St. Lawrence, M.L. McGrath, M.E. Oakley, & S.C. Sult, *Stress Management Training For Law Students: Cognitive-behavioral Intervention*, 1(4) Behavioral Sciences And The Law 101 (1983); P. Miller, *Personality Differences And Student Survival In Law School*, 19 Journal Of Legal Education 460 (1967); D.C. Moss, *Lawyer Personality*, 77(2) ABA Journal 34 (1991); P. Reidinger, *It's 46.5 Hours A Week In Law*, 72(9) ABA Journal 44 (1986); J.M. Rhoads, *Overwork*, 24 Journal of the American Medical Association 2615 (1977); Lawrence Richard, *The Lawyer Types*, 79(7) ABA Journal 74 (1993); H.I. Russek & L. Russek, *Is Emotional Stress An Etiological Factor In Coronary Heart Disease?*, 17 Psychosomatics 63 (1976); R.S. Smith, *A Profile Of Lawyer Lifestyles*, 70(2) ABA Journal 50 (1984); N. Solkoff & J. Markowitz, *Personality Characteristics Of First Year Medical And Law Students*, 42 Journal Of Medical Education 195 (1967); R. Tomasic, *Social Organization Amongst Australian Lawyers*, 19(3) Australian and New Zealand Journal of Sociology 447 (1983).

[22] Deborah L. Arron, Running From The Law 27, 39(1991); Walt Bachman, Law v. Life 100 (1995); Mary Ann Glendon, A Nation Under Lawyers 29 (1994); Anthony T. Kronman, The Lost Lawyer 300 (1993); Sol M. Linowitz & Martin Mayer, The Betrayed Profession: Lawyering At The End Of The Twentieth Century 107 (1994); Benjamin Sells, The Soul of the Law 71 (1994).

[23] John W. Wright, The American Almanac Of Jobs And Salaries 236 (1993).

[24] Lawrence R. Richard, *The Lawyer Types*, 79(7) ABA Journal 74 (1993); Lawrence R. Richard, Psychological Type And Job Satisfaction Among Practicing Lawyers In The United States (1994; Ph.D. dissertation, Temple Univ., Philadelphia, available through University Microfilms International Dissertation Services.)

[25] Mary Ann Glendon, A Nation Under Lawyers (1994); Anthony T. Kronman, The Lost Lawyer (1993); Sol M. Linowitz & Martin Mayer, The Betrayed Profession: Lawyering At The End Of The Twentieth Century (1994); Mike Papantonio, In Search Of Atticus Finch: A Motivational Book For Lawyers (1996); Benjamin Sells, The Soul of the Law (1994).

[26] Sharyn R. Anleau, *Women In Law:Theory, Research And Practice,* 28(3) Australian And New Zealand Journal Of Sociology 391 (1992); Fiona M. Kay & John Hagan, *The Persistent Glass Ceiling: Gendered Inequalities In The Earnings Of Lawyers,* 46(2) British Journal Of Sociology 279 (1995); Patricia MacCorquodale & Gary Jensen, *Women In The Law: Partners Or Tokens?,* 7(4) Gender And Society 582 (1993); Janet Rosenberg, Harry Perlstadt & William Phillips, *Now That We Are Here: Discrimination. Disparagement And Harassment At Work And The Experience Of Women Lawyers,* 7(3) Gender And Society 415 (1993).

[27] American Bar Association, The State Of The Legal Profession - 1984: Report Of The Young Lawyers Division (1985).

[28] American Bar Association, The State Of The Legal Profession - 1990: Report Of The Young Lawyers Division (1991).

[29] Monica Bay, *Life, Law And The Pursuit of Balance,* 20(4) Barrister Magazine 4 (1994).

[30] American Bar Association, ABA Young Lawyers Division Survey: Career Satisfaction (1995).

[31] North Carolina Bar Association, Quality of Life Survey of North Carolina Attorneys: Report of Quality of Life Task Force (1991).

[32] Lawrence R. Richard, *The Lawyer Types*, 79(7) ABA Journal 74 (1993); Lawrence R. Richard, Psychological Type And Job Satisfaction Among Practicing Lawyers In The United States (1994; Ph.D. dissertation, Temple Univ., Philadelphia, available through University Microfilms International Dissertation Services.); Contrary to a viewpoint that is

prevalent among lawyers, people who are more sensitive to emotional issues are not less intelligent. In fact, as I argue later in this book, just the opposite may be true.

[33] American Bar Association, The State Of The Legal Profession - 1990: Report Of The Young Lawyers Division (1991); American Bar Association, ABA Young Lawyers Division Survey: Career Satisfaction (1995); North Carolina Bar Association, Quality of Life Survey of North Carolina Attorneys: Report of Quality of Life Task Force (1991); Also, see preceding chapter.

[34] Joan Kofodimos, Balancing Act (1993); Anne W. Schaef & Diane Fassel, The Addictive Organization (1990); Karen C. Seybold and Paul R. Salamone, *Understanding Workaholsim; A Review Of Causes And Counseling Approaches*, 73(1) Journal of Counseling and Development 4 (1994).

[35] American Bar Association, The State Of The Legal Profession - 1990: Report Of The Young Lawyers Division (1991); Lawrence R. Richard, Psychological Type And Job Satisfaction Among Practicing Lawyers In The United States (1994; Ph.D. dissertation, Temple Univ., Philadelphia, available through University Microfilms International Dissertation Services).

[36] American Bar Association, The State Of The Legal Profession - 1990: Report Of The Young Lawyers Division (1991).

[37] Isaiah M. Zimmerman, *Stress And The Trial Lawyer,* 9(4) Litigation 37 (1983).

[38] Deborah Eisel, *How Do You Spell Relief: Family Lawyers Share Their Best Stress-Reduction Secrets*, 16(3) Family Advocate 16 (1994).

[39] This model of stress is based on the ideas of a number of theorists and researchers. See, Aaron T. Beck, Cognitive Therapy And Emotional Disorders (1976); Edward A. Charlesworth & Ronald G. Nathan, Stress Management (1984); Cary L. Cooper, Handbook Of Stress, Medicine, And Health (1995); Albert Ellis, Reason and Emotion In Psychotherapy (1962); J.J. Hurrell, L.R. Murphy, S.L. Sauter, & C.L. Cooper, Occupational stress: Issues and Developments in Research (1988); R.L. Kahn, & P. Byosiere, Stress in Organizations, In Handbook of Industrial and Organizational Psychology 571 (Vol.3, 2nd ed 1992); R.S. Lazarus & S. Folkman, Stress, Appraisal and Coping (1984); Richard S. Lazarus & Bernice N. Lazarus, Passion and Reason (1994); Hans Selye, History and Present Status of the Stress Concept, In Handbook of Stress 7 (1982); James C. Quick, Lawrence R. Murphy and Joseph J. Hurrell, Stress And Well-Being At Work: Assessments And Interventions For Occupational Mental Health (1992).

[40] Actually, at times even the first element of the stress response comes from within, in that our own thoughts, memories, emotional reactions and behaviors can themselves become stimuli.

[41] Bill Moyers, Healing and the Mind 177-247 (1993)

[42] Donald Bakal, Psychology & Health (1992); Cary L. Cooper, Handbook Of Stress, Medicine And Health (1995); Bill Moyers, Healing and the Mind (1993); Marc Schabracq, James A.M. Winnubst and Cary L. Cooper, Handbook Of Work And Health Psychology (1996); Charles Sheridan and Sally Radmacher, Health Psychology (1992); Shelley E. Taylor, Health Psychology (1995).

[43] Martin E. P. Seligman, Learned Optimism (1992); Martin E.P. Seligman, What You Can Change And What You Can't: The Complete Guide To Self-Improvement (1994); Christopher Peterson, Steven F. Maier and Martin E.P. Seligman, Learned Helplessness: A Theory For The Age Of Personal Control (1993).

[44] Donald Bakal, Psychology & Health 106-131(1992); Bill Moyers, Healing and the Mind 195-237 (1993); Charles Sheridan and Sally Radmacher, Health Psychology 74-85 (1992).

[45] Michael G. Goldstein & Raymond Niaura, Psychological Factors Affecting Physical Condition: Cardiovascular Disease Literature Review, 33(2) *Psychosomatics* 134 (1992); Andrew B. Littman, Review Of Psychosomatic Aspects of Cardiovascular Disease, 60 *Psychotherapy and Psychosomatics* 148 (1993).

[46] Herbert Benson, The Relaxation Response (1975).

[47] American Bar Association, At The Breaking Point (1991); Commission On Women In The Profession, Lawyers And Balanced Lives: A Guide To Drafting And Implementing Workplace Policies For Lawyers (1990).

[48] See, e.g., the September 16, 1996, issue of Business Week magazine.

[49] Edward Charlesworth and Ronald Nathan, Stress Management 47-165 (1984).

[50] E.g., Herbert Benson, The Relaxation Response (1975); Herbert Benson, Beyond The Relaxation Response (1984); Herbert Benson & Eileen Stuart, The Wellness Book: The Comprehensive Guide To Maintaining Health And Treating Stress-Related Illness (1992).

[51] Martha Davis, Elizabeth Robbins Eshelman and Mathew McKay, The Relaxation & Stress Reduction Workbook (1995).

[52] New Harbinger Publications, Inc., 5674 Shattuck Avenue, Oakland, CA 94609, (800) 748-6243.

[53] E.g., Edward Charlesworth and Ronald Nathan, Stress Management 47-165 (1984).

[54] E.g., Patricia Carrington, How To Relax (Random House Sound Editions 1985); Robert H. Reiner, How To Manage Stress (Random House Sound Editions 1983).

[55] See, e.g., David G. Myers, The Pursuit of Happiness: Who Is Happy-and Why (1992).

[56]Lawrence Richard, *The Lawyer Types*, 79(7) ABA Journal 74 (1993).

[57] Daniel Goleman, Emotional Intelligence (1995).

[58] Richard S. Lazarus & Bernice N. Lazarus, Passion and Reason (1994).

[59] G.A.H. Benjamin, A. Kaszniak, B.D. Sales & S.B. Shanfield, *The Role Of Legal Education In Producing Psychological Distress Among Law Students And Lawyers*, American Bar Foundation Research Journal 225 (1986); R. Frances, G. Alexopoulos, & V. Yandow, *Lawyers' Alcoholism*, 4(2) Advances In Alcohol And Substance Abuse 59 (1984); Forsyth & T.J. Danisiewicz, *Toward A Theory Of Professionalization*, 12(1) Work and Occupations 59 (1985);M.D. Gupta, *Machiavellianism Of Different Occupational Groups*, 18(2) Indian Journal of Psychometry and Education 61 (1987); J.P. Heinz & E.O. Laumann, Chicago Lawyers: The Social Structure of the Bar (1984); S. Reich, *California Psychological Inventory: Profile Of A Sample Of First Year Law Students*, 38 Psychological Reports 871 (1976); N. Solkoff & J. Markowitz, *Personality Characteristics Of First Year Medical And Law Students*, 42 Journal Of Medical Education 195 (1967); R. Tomasic, *Social Organization Amongst Australian Lawyers*, 19(3) Australian and New Zealand Journal of Sociology 447 (1983).

[60] Redford Williams, The Trusting Heart (1989); Redford Williams & Virginia Williams, Anger Kills (1993).

[61] J.C. Barefoot, K.A. Dodge, B.L. Peterson, W.G. Dahlstrom & R.B. Williams, *The Cook-Medley Hostility Scale: Item Content And Ability To Predict Survival,* 51 Psychosomatic Medicine 46 (1989).

[62] Donald Bakal, Psychology & Health 106-131(1992); Bill Moyers, Healing and the Mind 195-237 (1993); Charles Sheridan and Sally Radmacher, Health Psychology 74-85 (1992).

[63] Sol M. Linowitz & Martin Mayer, The Betrayed Profession: Lawyering At The End Of The Twentieth Century (1994).

[64]Comprehensive Alcohol Abuse and Alcoholism Prevention, Treatment, and Rehabilitation Act, 42 U.S.C. §4582, transferred to the Public Health Service Act, 42 U.S.C.A. §290dd-2 (Supp. 1993); Drug Abuse Prevention, Treatment, and Rehabilitation Act, 21 U.S.C. §1175, transferred to the Public Health Service Act, 42 U.S.C.A. §290dd-2 (Supp. 1993); see also 38 U.S.C.A. §7332 (Supp. 1992) [Veteran's Administration Hospitals].

[65]E.g., American Psychological Association, *Ethical Principles of Psychologists and Code of Conduct*, 47 Am. Psychol. 1597 (1992).

[66]E.g., 42 Pa. Stat. Ann. §§5929, 5944, 5945, 5945.1, 5948 (Purdon 1993).

[67]*Jaffe v. Redmond*, 116 S.Ct. __, 64 U.S.L.W. 4490 (June 13, 1996).

[68]See, e.g., *Pennsylvania Mental Health Procedures Act*, 50 Pa. Stat. Ann §§7101, 7111 (Purdon 1969 & Supp. 1993); 42 U.S.C.A. §290dd-2.

[69]See, e.g., West's Legal News, *Missouri Bar Hires Full-Time Substance-Abuse Counselor*, 1996 WL 257755 (Jan. 1996); Angie Fought, *Help for Addicted Lawyers*, 18 Pa. Lawyer 32 (March/April 1996).

[70] See, e.g., Tennessee Supreme Court Rules, 9, §28.1(g) (1993); Tennessee Code Ann. §§ 23.4.104, 23.4.105 (1993); Texas Health and Safety Code Ann. § 467.007 (Vernon 1992).

[71]42 C.F.R. §§2.1, 2.31(a) (rev. 10/1/92) [substance abuse information]; e.g., 55 Pa. Code §5100.34(d)-(f) [mental health information].

[72] "This information has been disclosed to you from records protected by Federal confidentiality rules (42 CFR part 2). The Federal rules prohibit you from making any further disclosure of this information unless further disclosure is expressly permitted by the written consent of the person to whom it pertains or as otherwise permitted by 42 CFR part 2. A general authorization for the release of medical or other information is NOT sufficient for this purpose. The Federal rules restrict any use of the information to criminally investigate or prosecute any alcohol or drug abuse patient." 42 C.F.R. §2.32.

[73]For example, in Pennsylvania, the following provision must accompany mental health information that is released from inpatient or involuntary outpatient settings: "This information has been disclosed to you from records whose confidentiality is protected by State statute. State regulations limit your right to make any further disclosure of this information without prior written consent of the person to whom it pertains." 55 Pa. Code §5100.34(d).

[74] See, e.g., Medical Society of New Jersey v. Jacobs, Civ. A. No. 93-3670 (WGB), 1993 WL 413016, (D. N.J. Oct. 5, 1993); Ellen S. v. Florida Board of Bar Examiners, Case No. 94-0429, 1994 U.S. Dist. LEXIS 10842 (S.D. Fla. 1994); Clark v. Virginia Board of Bar Examiners, No. 94-211-A, 1994 WL 364443 (E.D. Va. 1994).

[75] P.L. 101-336, 42 U.S.C. §§12101 *et seq.* (1990).

[76] See generally John Parry, Mental Disability Law: A Primer (American Bar Association Commission on Mental and Physical Disability Law, 1995); John Parry, Regulation, Litigation and Dispute Resolution Under the American with Disabilities Act (American Bar Association Commission on Mental and Physical Disability Law, 1996).

[77]See generally Carl Anderson, Thomas McCracken, & Betty Reddy, *Addictive Illness in the Legal Profession: Bar Examiners Dilemma*, Professional Lawyer 16 (May 1996).

[78]P.L. 101-336, 42 U.S.C. §§12101 *et seq.* (1990).

[79]29 U.S.C. §794.

[80]*In Re Applications of Anne Underwood and Judith Ann Plano*, 1993 WL 649283 (Dec. 7, 1993).

[81]42 U.S.C. §12119; see, e.g., 14 Mental and Physical Disability Law Rptr 65 (Sept. 1996); see also Wayne F. Cascio, *The Americans With Disabilities Act of 1990 and the 1991 Civil Rights Act: Requirements for Psychological Practice in the Work Place, in* Psychology in Litigation and Legislation (Julie Blackman, Wayne F. Casio, Stephen J. Ceci, Gary B. Melton, & Michael O. Miller, eds., American Psychological Association, 1994).

[82]42 U.S.C. §12210; see generally Nancy Jones, *The Alcohol and Drug Provisions of the ADA: Implications for Employers and Employees, in* Implications of the Americans with Disabilities Act for Psychology 151 (Susan M. Bruyere and Janet O'Keeffe, eds., American Psychological Association, 1994).

[83]H. Conf. Rep. No. 596, 101st Cong., 2d Sess., at 64.

[84]U.S. Equal Employment Opportunity Commission, A Technical Assistance Manual on the Employment Provisions of the Americans with Disabilities Act §II-3 (1992).

[85]E.g., Jeffrey J. Fleury, Comment, *Kicking the Habit: Diversion in Michigan - The Sensible Approach*, 73 U. Det. Mercy L. Rev. 11 (1995); Jody Luna, Report of the Medical Evaluation Subcommittee of the Colorado Supreme Court Grievance Committee, Presentation at the 8th National Workshop for Lawyer Assistance Programs (Sponsored by the American Bar Association Commission on Impaired Attorneys, Sept. 11-14, 1995).

[86]E.g., 204 Pa. Code §§89.151, 89.291; for a contrary opinion, see Hamilton P. Fox, *Alcoholic Lawyers: Are They Being Coddled By Attorney Discipline Systems?*, 82 A.B.A. J. 38 (Jan. 1996).

[87]*In Re B. Franklin Kersey.*, 520 A.2d 321 (D.C. App. 1987); see generally Jonathan Goodliffe, *Alcohol and Depression in English and American Lawyer Disciplinary Proceedings*, 89 Addiction 1237 (1994); Patricia Sue Heil, *Tending the Bar in Texas: Alcoholism as a Mitigating Factor in Attorney Discipline,* 24(4) St. Mary's law Journal 1263 (1993).

[88]E.g., 204 Pa. Code §89.293(a); see also *Office of Disciplinary Counsel v. Braun*, 553 A.2d 894 (Pa. 1989).

[89]ABA Manual on Professional Conduct §131:3202; ABA Standards for Imposing Lawyer Sanctions, standard 9.32(i) (Feb. 4, 1992).

[90]42 C.F.R. §2.35(a).

[91]See generally Mary Melissa Lucas, Comment, *Rehabilitation, Mitigation, and Reform in Dealing with Chemically Impaired Attorneys*, 21 Cap. U. L. Rev. 889, 907-908 (1992).

[92]American Bar Association, Model Law Firm/Legal Department Personnel Impairment Policy and Guidelines §1.5 (1990).

[93]P.L. 101-336, 42 U.S.C. §§12101 *et seq.* (1990).

[94]42 U.S.C. §12119; see, e.g., 14 Mental and Physical Disability Law Rptr 65 (Sept. 1996); see also Wayne F. Cascio, *The Americans With Disabilities Act of 1990 and the 1991 Civil Rights Act: Requirements for Psychological Practice in the Work Place, in* Psychology in Litigation and Legislation (Julie Blackman, Wayne F. Casio, Stephen J. Ceci, Gary B. Melton, & Michael O. Miller, eds., American Psychological Association, 1994).

[95] North Carolina Bar Association, Quality of Life Survey of North Carolina Attorneys: Report of Quality of Life Task Force (1991).

[96] G.A.H. Benjamin, E.J. Darling & B.D. Sales, *The Prevalence of Depression, Alcohol Abuse, And Cocaine Abuse Among United States Lawyers,* 13 International Journal of Law and Psychiatry 233 (1990).

[97]G. Andrew, H. Benjamin, Elaine J. Darling, & Bruce Sales, *The Prevalence of Depression, Alcohol Abuse, and Cocaine Abuse Among United States Lawyers*, 13 Int'l J. Law & Psychiatry 233, 241 (1990); Eric Drogan, *Alcoholism in the Legal Profession: Psychological and Legal Perspectives and Interventions*, 15 Law & Psychol. Rev. 117, 127 (1991); Stephanie B. Goldberg, *Drawing the Line: When is an Ex-Coke Addict Fit to Practice Law?*, A.B.A. J. 50 (Feb. 1990); see also Angie Fought, *Help for Addicted Lawyers,* 18 Pa. Lawyer 29 (March/April 1996); Jeffrey J. Fleury, Comment, *Kicking the Habit: Diversion in Michigan - The Sensible Approach*, 73 U. Det. Mercy L. Rev. 11, 14 (1995).

[98]E.g., Michael A. Bloom & Carol Lynn Wallinger, *Lawyers and Alcoholism: Is it Time for a New Approach?*, 61 Temple L.Rev. 1409 (1988); Laurie B. Dowell, *Attorneys and Alcoholism: An Alternative Approach to a Serious Problem*, 16 N. Ky. L.Rev. 169 (1988); Patricia Sue Heil, Comment, *Tending the Bar in Texas: Alcoholism as a Mitigating Factor in Attorney Discipline*, 24 St. Mary's L.J. 1263, 1265 (1993).

[99]E.g., Terence Williams, "I Won't Wait Up Tonight" (Hazelton Educational Materials, 1992).

[100]American Psychiatric Association, Diagnostic and Statistical Manual of Mental Disorders, at 181, 182-83 (4th ed., 1994).

[101]William R. Miller & Stephen Rollnick, Motivational Interviewing: Preparing People to Change Addictive Behavior (1991)

[102]See G. Alan Marlatt & Judith R. Gordon, Relapse Prevention: Maintenance Strategies in the Treatment of Addictive Behaviors (1985); Dennis L. Thombs, Introduction to Addictive Behaviors (1994).

[103]E.g., Ralph E. Tarter, Howard B. Moss, & Michael M. Vanyukov, *Behavioral Genetics and the Etiology of Alcoholism, in* The Genetics of Alcoholism (Vol. 1) (1995); Richard Rende & Robert Plomin, *Diathesis-Stress Models of Psychopathology*, 1 Appl. & Prevent. Psychol. 177 (1992).

[104]Robert M. Anthenelli & Marc A. Schuckit, *Genetics, in* Substance Abuse: A Comprehensive Textbook - 2d ed. (Joyce H. Lowinson, Pedro Ruiz, Robert B. Millman, & John G. Langrod, eds. 1992).

[105]E.g., Patti Juliana & Carolyn Goodman, *Children of Substance Abusing Parents, in* Substance Abuse: A Comprehensive Textbook - 2d ed. (Joyce H. Lowinson, Pedro Ruiz, Robert B. Millman, & John G. Langrod, eds. 1992).

[106]Edward J. Khantzian, Kurt S. Halliday, & William E. McAuliffe, Addiction and the Vulnerable Self (1990).

[107]E.g., Boris Tabakoff & Paula L. Hoffman, *Alcohol: Neurobiology,* Substance Abuse: A Comprehensive Textbook - 2d ed. (Joyce H. Lowinson, Pedro Ruiz, Robert B. Millman, & John G. Langrod, eds. 1992); Stephen A. Maisto, Mark Galizio, & Gerard J. Connors, Drug Use and Misuse (1991).

[108]Marc Galanter & Herbert D. Kleber, The American Psychiatric Press Textbook of Substance Abuse Treatment (1994).

[109]See Dennis L. Thombs, Introduction to Addictive Behaviors (1994); Marc Alan Schuckit, Educating Yourself About Alcohol and Drug Problems: A People's Primer (1995).

[110]American Psychiatric Association, *Practice Guideline for Treatment of Patients with Substance Use Disorders: Alcohol, Cocaine, Opioids* (1995); Rebecca Schilit & Edith S. Lisansky Gomberg, Drugs and Behavior: A Sourcebook for the Helping Professions (1991).

[111]See, e.g., Peter M. Monti, David B. Abrams, Ronald M. Kadden, & Ned L. Cooney, Treating Alcohol Dependence: A Coping Skills Training Guide (1989).

[112]American Psychiatric Association, *Practice Guideline for Treatment of Patients with Substance Use Disorders: Alcohol, Cocaine, Opioids* (1995).

[113]See, e.g., Stephen A. Maisto, Mark Galizio, & Gerard J. Connors, Drug Use and Misuse (1991).

[114]Albert Ellis, John F. McInerney, Raymond DiGiuseppe, & Raymond J. Yeager, Rational-Emotive Therapy with Alcoholics and Substance Abusers (1988).

[115]Timothy J. O'Farrell (ed.), Treating Alcohol Problems: Marital and Family Interventions (1993).

[116]Compare, e.g., William R. Miller & Ricardo F. Munoz, How to Control Your Drinking (rev. ed., 1982).

[117]See Barbara S. McCrady & William R. Miller (eds.), Research on Alcoholics Anonymous (1993).

[118] Edgar P. Nace, *Alcoholics Anonymous,* in Substance Abuse: A Comprehensive Textbook (Joyce H. Lowinson, Pedro Ruiz, Robert B. Millman & John G. Langrod, eds. 1992).

[119] North Carolina Bar Association, Quality of Life Survey of North Carolina Attorneys: Report of Quality of Life Task Force (1991).

[120] G.A.H. Benjamin, E.J. Darling & B.D. Sales, *The Prevalence of Depression, Alcohol Abuse, And Cocaine Abuse Among United States Lawyers,* 13 International Journal of Law and Psychiatry 233 (1990).

[121] W.W. Eaton, J.C. Anthony, W. Mandel & R. Garrison, *Occupations And The Prevalence Of Major Depressive Disorder,* 32 Journal Of Occupational Medicine 1079 (1990).

[122] Robert M. Carney, Kenneth E. Freedland, Michael W. Rich & Allan S. Jaffe, *Depression As A Risk Factor For Cardiac Events In Established Coronary Heart Disease: A Review Of Possible Mechanisms,* 17(2) Annals Of Behavioral Medicine 142 (1995); Andrew B. Littman, *Review of Psychosomatic Aspects of Cardiovascular Disease,* 60 Psychotherapy And Psychosomatics 148 (1993).

[123] Arthur Shwartz and Ruth M. Schwartz, Depression: Theories and Treatments - Psychological, Biological and Social Perspectives (1993).

[124] David O. Antonuccio, William G. Danton & Garland YY. DeNelsky, *Psychotherapy Versus Medication For Depression: Challenging The Conventional Wisdom With Data,* 26(6) Professional Psychology: Research and Practice 574 (1995).

[125] Aaron Beck, A. John Rush, Brain F. Shaw & Gary Emery, Cognitive Therapy Of Depression (1979); Albert Ellis, Reason And Emotion In Psychotherapy (1994).

[126] David O. Antonuccio, William G. Danton & Garland YY. DeNelsky, *Psychotherapy Versus Medication For Depression: Challenging The Conventional Wisdom With Data,* 26(6) Professional Psychology: Research and Practice 574 (1995).

[127] Sidney J. Blatt, *The Destructiveness of Perfectionism,* 50 American Psychologist 1003 (1995).

[128] American Bar Association, At The Breaking Point: The Report Of A National Conference On The Emerging Crisis In The Quality Of Lawyers' Health And Lives, And Its Impact On Law Firms And Client Services (1991); American Bar Association, The State Of The Legal Profession - 1990: Report Of The Young Lawyers Division (1991).

[129] Alec Mackenzie, The Time Trap 55 (1990).

[130] Two of the best time management books in print are: Stephen R. Covey, A. Roger Merrill and Rebecca R. Merrill, First Things First (1994); Alec Mackenzie, The Time Trap (1990). In particular, Mackenzie's book is filled with the types of specific behavioral tips discussed in this chapter.

[131] E.g., Kenneth Blanchard and Spencer Johnson, The One Minute Manager (1982); Alec Mackenzie, The Time Trap 104 (1990).

[132] Two of the best time management books in print are: Stephen R. Covey, A. Roger Merrill and Rebecca R. Merrill, First Things First (1994); Alec Mackenzie, The Time Trap (1990).

[133] Stephen R. Covey, A. Roger Merrill and Rebecca R. Merrill, First Things First (1994).

[134] Some have attributed this quote to Ralph Waldo Emerson, while others claim it to be the words of Bessie Anderson Stanley. After hours of research and the help of many librarians, I have discovered that no one seems to be certain about its origin. However, it is the thought that counts.

[135] D. Von Drehle, *The Crumbling Of A Pillar In Washington,* The Washington Post A20 (Aug. 15, 1993). Quote also appears in Sidney J. Blatt, *The Destructiveness of Perfectionism,* 50 American Psychologist 1003 (1995).

[136] Suzanne C. Kobasa, *Commitment and Coping in Stress Resistance Among Lawyers,* 42(4) Journal of Personality and Social Psychology 707 (1982); Mary E. Sweetman, David C. Munz & Robert J. Wheeler, *Optimism, Hardiness, and Explanatory Style as Predictors of General Well Being Among Attorneys,* 29 Social Indicators Research 153 (1993).

[137] J.C. Barefoot, K.A. Dodge, B.L. Peterson, W.G. Dahlstrom & R.B. Williams, *The Cook-Medley Hostility Scale: Item Content And Ability To Predict Survival,* 51 Psychosomatic Medicine 46 (1989).

[138] David G. Myers, The Pursuit of Happiness: Who Is Happy - and Why (1992).

[139] Stephen R. Covey, The 7 Habits Of Highly Effective People (1989).

ORDER FORM : *"STRESS MANAGEMENT FOR LAWYERS-2nd ed."*

ORDER BY MAIL, FAX OR PHONE

MAIL: Vorkell Group, Box 447
Gwynedd, PA 19436

FAX: (215) 661-9328

PHONE: (800) 759-1222

- # of Copies _____ @ $19.95 = $ _____
- Volume Discount .... _____
  (6-23 copies = 20%, > 23 copies = 30%)
- PA Residents Add 6% Sales Tax ... _____
- Shipping Costs.................... _____
  ($2.50 First Book, $.50 Each Additional)
- TOTAL DUE .... _____

Allow 1-2 weeks for shipping. To receive books in 3 days simply write "RUSH" on form and include $4 for first book and $1 for each additional book. Please note that prices shown on this form are subject to change with periodic rises in costs.

SHIP MY ORDER TO:

_____

_____

_____

NOTE: If P.O. Box Number, also indicate street address if possible.

Phone: _____

CHOOSE PAYMENT METHOD:

☐ Check   ☐ MasterCard   ☐ VISA   ☐ Amer. Exp.

Card#: ____ — ____ — ____ — ____

Exp. Date: ____ / ____

Cardholder's Signature: _____